Yesterday
Once More

Memories of the Carpenters
and Their Music

Yesterday Once More

Memories of the Carpenters and Their Music

Edited by Randy Schmidt

Tiny Ripple Books
P.O. Box 1533
Cranberry Township, PA 16066

Published by:
Tiny Ripple Books
P.O. Box 1533
Cranberry Township, PA 16066
www.tinyripple.com
ISBN 0-9675973-1-5
Library of Congress Catalog Card Number: 00-107985
Printed in the United States of America
See page 237 for a list of copyright permissions and photo credits

For my mom Linda

Contents

Part Two: Top Of The World

Part Three: There's A Kind Of Hush

Part Four: Rainy Days And Mondays

Part Five: A Song For You

Preface

This is the first Carpenters book of its kind – a history book of sorts, in the making for over thirty years. Featuring the thoughts and words of journalists and critics, as well as Karen and Richard themselves, this is a collection of more than 40 articles, essays, interviews, reviews, and reassessments. The Carpenters are well suited to this pointillism-style biography. Their happiness and heartbreak, their triumphs and tragedies were all recorded on the pages of magazines and newspapers all around the world.

Varying perspectives and opinions on the group were intentionally chosen for inclusion here in order to convey a sense of how the Carpenters were viewed in the press during their heyday – and how they were rediscovered during the 1990s. Through the years, they had cynics questioning (even occasionally attacking) them, and they had some eloquent defenders.

Writers such as Paul Grein, Tom Nolan, Ray Coleman, John Tobler, and Robert Hilburn explore the artistry of the Carpenters in critical assessments. Scholarly essays from music authorities such as Frank Pooler and Daniel Levitin analyze the technical elements of the group's innovative vocal and instrumental arrangements. Extensive interviews with Karen and Richard provide the duo's own assessment of their music, their goals, and their image. Reviews from *Variety* and other sources trace the Carpenters' concerts from their early Vegas shows to their concert hall triumphs (such as the 1976 London Palladium engagement), and all the way through to Richard's most recent solo performances.

In addition to analyses from respected music industry publications such as *Billboard, Rolling Stone*, and *Melody Maker*, this book includes some rather lightweight articles from entertainment- or teen-oriented magazines such as *TV Radio Mirror* and *Star*. Also included are a number of articles from *The Southeast News* and other local Downey, California newspapers, which offer a unique "hometown" perspective on the Carpenters.

Researching and collecting published material on the Carpenters has been a continuous pursuit for me over the past decade or so. For years I have visited public and college libraries, rummaging through dusty shelves and scrolling through what had to be miles of microfilm and microfiche in hopes of finding even one more piece of the puzzle. It wasn't until recently that I realized that some of the best and most insightful articles on the Carpenters had been out of widespread circulation for years (and some never received wide circulation in the first place).

You should be aware that the selections I am introducing (or in most cases *reintroducing*) here are not always word-for-word reproductions of the original pieces. Although I have made every effort to maintain the content and essence of each one, they have been edited for the purpose of creating a better, reader-friendly book.

This archival history of Karen and Richard Carpenter is intended to entertain and inform both the Carpenters neophyte and diehard Carpentersphile. It is hoped that, collectively, these articles will provide insight as to why the Carpenters continue to garner new fans, and why their music seems to gain more respect the more it is reexamined.

Randy Schmidt

Acknowledgments

Assembling this book would have been an impossible task if it weren't for the generosity and assistance of many wonderful people. From Los Angeles to New York, England to Japan (and many places in-between), Carpenters enthusiasts, journalists, librarians and others have been eager to assist in my quest to compile this history of the Carpenters... one precious piece at a time.

My editor and publisher, Jeff Bleiel of Tiny Ripple Books, deserves the greatest recognition. In addition to his expertise, creativity and patience, Jeff has been there every step of the way, answering my many questions and always keeping me grounded and on task. He is even responsible for locating several of the pieces presented here. Most of all I thank Tiny Ripple Books for giving me the exciting opportunity to bring this book to life.

On the home front, my wife Jennifer and daughter Camryn have been so supportive and patient during the construction of this book. My parents and family also warrant "thanks" for encouraging and tolerating my many ventures over the years.

My appreciation also goes out to Jim Ogrady at the Downey City Library for his endless support. His research assistance at the library and Downey Historical Society unearthed several rare and essential items included in this collection.

Thanks to Laura Adam, David Alley and Alley Management, Rich Archbold and the *Long Beach Press-Telegram*, Carolyn Arzac, Robert Autenrieth and Star Shots, Ken Bertwell, Barry Bilicki and the Carpenters Photo Page, Joe Bine, Hal Blaine, Dana Britten-Stein, Ron Bunt, Rick Cybul, Donnie Demers, Digby Diehl, Andrew G. Doe, Cami Elen and Interscope/Geffen/A&M Records, Miyuki Fujiwara, Dean Gautschy, Julie Gonzales, Elizabeth Gorzelany, Paul Grein, Sue Gustin, Robert Ingves, June Jones, Joshua Kessler, Patti Kistler, David Konjoyan, Jon Konjoyan, Randy Kosht, Peter Lesnik and the Carpenter Performing Arts Center, Ambrose Martin, Joel McNally, Ken Michaels, Ann Moats, Nancy Naglin, Erica Nemmers, Yuko Ogura, Gordon Pogoda, Frank Pooler, Richard Ramirez, Neil Rudish and the A&M Corner Forum, Greg Rule, Victoria Sarinelli, Kala Schaap, Norma Segarra, Steve Sidoruk, Tierney Smith, Ron Spagnardi, Michelle Blaine Stoneman, John Tobler, Charlie Tuna, Ethlie Ann Vare, Evelyn Wallace and Paul Williams.

I thank you for your interest in this book and hope you find it to be a valuable resource and an enjoyable read. Most especially, I am grateful to Karen and Richard Carpenter for their inexhaustible drive and ability to create captivating music and for the enjoyment it continues to provide after all these years.

Randy Schmidt
September 2000

Prelude

The Carpenters Story

By Paul Grein

More than thirty years after their breakthrough, the Carpenters rank among the most popular acts in recording history. Their worldwide sales top 100 million copies. Their many honors include three Grammy Awards, an American Music Award, a star on the Hollywood Walk of Fame, two recordings in the Grammy Hall of Fame and enough gold and platinum records to fill a museum.

The Carpenters were the #1 American-born hit-makers of the 1970s, according to Joel Whitburn's authoritative *Top Pop Singles*. From "(They Long To Be) Close To You" in 1970 to "Only Yesterday" in 1975, they never missed the Top 15. And their success went far beyond their homeland: Karen and Richard topped the charts from Holland to Hong Kong.

Though they recorded as the Carpenters for just 13 years, Karen and Richard made a deep and lasting impact. They have been cited as a key influence by such varied acts as k.d. lang, Sonic Youth, Madonna, Luther Vandross and Shania Twain. Recent compilations of their hits have become best sellers in Japan, the U.K. and the U.S.

The Carpenters were, at various points, hot and cold; adored and scorned. But Karen and Richard came out on top in the end. Their recordings are now regarded as classics. Their sound is considered timeless.

If you made a checklist of the qualities of a great singer, Karen Carpenter had them all: tremendous presence, a natural, conversational ease, and impeccable intonation and control.

But as strong as Karen was from a technical standpoint, it was the emotion she communicated that made her so compelling. Karen had a knack for peeling away the outer layers of a song and getting to its core. And once she located a song's essential truth, it was as if she were singing just to you.

In an interview with *The Los Angeles Times*, Herb Alpert, the co-founder of A&M Records, remembered the first time he heard a demo tape of Karen's voice: "It just jumped right out at me," Alpert said. "It felt like she was in the room with me." Alpert wasn't the only one who felt that way. The intimacy in Karen's voice allowed her to form a one-to-one bond with millions of fans all over the world.

Karen's style combined the most attractive traits of several other legendary American singers. She had the warm, pure tones of Nat "King" Cole, the clarity and precision of Barbra Streisand, and the vulnerability of Judy Garland. It was this last quality that most impressed the late Henry Mancini. "Karen had a quality about her that was so vulnerable, so exposed that she just demanded attention," he said. "Whatever she sang came right from the heart."

Karen was always natural and unpretentious – qualities that too often caused her to be taken for granted. Fortunately, in the years since Karen's death, she has received ever-increasing recognition as one of the most gifted pop vocalists of all time.

As the chief architect of the Carpenters' sound, Richard Carpenter arranged and orchestrated almost all of the duo's recordings. He produced most of them, composed many, and played keyboards on all but a few.

Richard received five Grammy nominations for his arrangements, recognizing his contributions to such signature Carpenters hits as "Close To You," "Superstar" and "Sing." Richard's arrangements have proved highly influential. His chart for "We've Only Just Begun," which blends the romanticism of easy listening with the pulse of pop/rock, provided a virtual blueprint for the modern adult contemporary format.

In addition to his work in the studio, Richard was always on the lookout for new material for the Carpenters. He spotted future hits in a wide range of sources, from a major Hollywood movie to a local TV commercial. Richard also teamed with lyricist John Bettis to write six Carpenters singles. Four of them reached the Top 10 in both the U.S. and the U.K.

In his *Rolling Stone* review of *The Singles 1969-1973*, critic Paul Gambaccini made note of Richard's role in the Carpenters' success. "Heard together, the duo's hits prove that Richard Carpenter didn't study music at Yale for nothing. His clean arrangements, delicate piano turns and conservatively employed strings enhance almost every cut, and after a few tracks it becomes obvious his contributions have been grossly underestimated."

Herb Alpert seconded the point in Ray Coleman's 1994 book, *The Carpenters: The Untold Story*. "He knew how to surround her voice with the right tapestry, the songs that would work best for her," Alpert said. "And he wouldn't settle for anything less than he thought was right."

After several years of auditions and rejections, the Carpenters signed with A&M Records in April 1969. They immediately commenced work on their debut album, *Offering*. The album was released six months later, but it made little impact until a single, "Ticket To Ride," took off in early 1970.

It's fitting that the Carpenters, who were Beatles fans from Day One, chose a Lennon/McCartney song as their first single. It's also characteristic of Karen and Richard that they didn't just record a sound-alike version to get a quick hit. That would have been too easy. Instead, Richard transformed the song from an up-tempo rocker to a melancholy ballad. The single, which climbed halfway up the *Billboard* chart, introduced many of the elements that would become signatures of the Carpenters sound.

Burt Bacharach admired the Carpenters' remake of "Ticket To Ride," and asked them to perform a medley of his songs at an upcoming benefit. Herb Alpert suggested they include "(They Long To Be) Close To You," which, despite recordings by Dionne Warwick and Dusty Springfield, had never become a hit. Richard didn't think the song was right for the medley, but Alpert was sure it was right for the Carpenters. He urged Karen and Richard to record it for their next album. Alpert was on to something. The Carpenters' light touch on "Close To You" was just right for the romantic creampuff. Karen's lead vocal is engagingly coquettish. Richard's slow-shuffle arrangement features a warm trumpet solo and a splash of mellow California harmonies. Bacharach, who arranged Warwick's 1964 recording of the song, was impressed. "I think Richard Carpenter really nailed the essence of the song," the pop titan says. The facts speak for themselves: Of the hundreds of outside cover versions of Bacharach songs to be released over the past 40 years, this is the only one to reach #1. "Close To You" received a Grammy nomination for Record of the Year and brought the Carpenters two Grammy Awards – Best New Artist of the Year and Best Contemporary Vocal Performance By a Group. In February 2000, the recording was voted into the Grammy Hall of Fame.

The Carpenters followed "Close To You" with another smash that quickly became their signature song. Richard spotted "We've Only Just Begun" on Los Angeles television – as a bank commercial. The Carpenters' recording turned it from a jingle into a standard: It received a Grammy nomination for Song of the Year and became the wedding song for a generation. The tale of a young couple just starting out is so idyllic that it could, in lesser hands, have seemed dewy and precious – like a Hallmark card set to music. The Carpenters made the story seem real. Richard's arrangement has energy and spunk. Karen's lead vocal conveys strength, optimism and a deep contentment. This recording was also voted into the Grammy Hall of Fame.

Both of these million-sellers were featured on the *Close To You* album, which was a Grammy finalist for Album of the Year. *Close To You* was also the first of five consecutive Carpenters albums to reach the Top 5 on the *Billboard* charts and to be certified multiplatinum.

Both artistically and commercially, Karen and Richard were at the peak of their game in 1971. Their *Carpenters* album spent nearly six months in the Top 10 and included three gold singles, "For All We Know," "Rainy Days And Mondays" and "Superstar."

"For All We Know" was the second wedding song in a row to become a Carpenters smash. But where "We've Only Just Begun" expresses romantic certainty, "For All We Know" conveys a measure of doubt and ambivalence. The single was in the Top 10 when the song, from the movie *Lovers And Other Strangers,* won an Academy Award.

Paul Williams and Roger Nichols, who wrote the blissful "We've Only Just Begun," also created the melancholy "Rainy Days And Mondays," one of the most nakedly emotional ballads ever to become a pop hit. Karen's bluesy vocal is a study in control, as she builds effortlessly from a conversational opening to a searing finish.

The Carpenters outdid themselves with their haunting recording of "Superstar." Richard's arrangement creates a chilling sense of foreboding. Karen's husky vocal heightens the drama. It's easy listening with an edge.

Carpenters brought Karen and Richard their second straight Grammy Award for Best Pop Performance by a Group – and their second straight nomination for Album of the Year.

The Carpenters had such an abundance of great material in 1971 that "Bless The Beasts And Children" was relegated to the B-side of "Superstar." Even so, it made the charts in its own right in December 1971. Karen projected both gentleness and strength on the ballad, which was the title song from a movie by producer Stanley Kramer. The Carpenters performed the Oscar-nominated song on the Academy Awards in April 1972.

Karen and Richard returned a few months later with *A Song For You,* which included an amazing five Top 15 singles. Richard and John Bettis co-wrote two of the biggest hits from the album, "Top Of The World" and "Goodbye To Love."

Richard's arrangement for "Goodbye To Love" is among his most inventive and influential. He envisioned the lament as a genre-bending tour-de-force, complete with a head-turning fuzz-guitar solo. Richard brought in a talented young guitarist, Tony Peluso, and asked him to play the melody for five bars – and then improvise. The result was not only a worldwide Top 10 hit, but also a new style: the "power lead" guitar solo in a ballad context. The long fade-out, complete with guitar, vocals and organ, has a majestic quality – making "Goodbye To Love" the "Hey Jude" of unrequited love songs.

A Song For You also included "Hurting Each Other," "It's Going To Take Some Time," and another Paul Williams-Roger Nichols song that has become a standard, "I Won't Last A Day Without You." The Carpenters' recording of the latter song won Japan's World Disc Grand Prix as Single of the Year in 1974. The poignant ballad was perfect for Karen's style and persona. It proved once again that in quality, if not in quantity of hits, the combination of the Carpenters and Williams/Nichols was to the early '70s what the Dionne Warwick and Bacharach/David tandem was to the '60s.

A sense of longing in Karen's voice came across even on happy songs such as "Sing." That gave the "Sesame Street" sing-a-long a faintly bittersweet quality, similar to Charles Chaplin's theme song, "Smile." Karen and Richard first heard "Sing," which had been a minor chart hit for Barbra Streisand, on the set of a TV special in January 1973. By late February, their version was headed for gold. It later brought them two Grammy nominations.

"Sing" was significant for another reason: It was the first recording on which Richard and Karen were officially credited as producers. The Carpenters featured the song on their 1973 album *Now & Then*, which spawned another gold hit in "Yesterday Once More." Richard and John Bettis wrote the wistful ballad in response to the nostalgia craze of the early '70s. The single went gold and reached #2 in both the U.S. and the U.K. It did even better in Japan, where it became one of the best-selling hits of all time.

Karen and Richard closed out the year with the release of *The Singles 1969-1973*. The album shot to No. 1 in both the U.S. and the U.K. The album topped the U.K. chart for 17 weeks – a total matched by only two other albums in the '70s: Simon & Garfunkel's *Bridge Over Troubled Water* and the *Saturday Night Fever* soundtrack.

By 1974, just about everyone knew that the Carpenters excelled at lyric-driven ballads. With "Please Mr. Postman," they proved they could also "deliver" with a rhythm-based oldie. Richard's taut, propulsive arrangement helped to update the Marvelettes classic; Karen's playful pout and spirited drumming added to its appeal. "Postman" reached #1 in the U.S. and #2 in the U.K. It also became a hit in the few countries that hadn't previously fallen under the Carpenters' spell. As a result, "Postman" became the duo's all-time top-selling international hit.

The follow-up, "Only Yesterday," is really two songs in one, with a poignant verse giving way to a zesty chorus. Richard and John Bettis wrote the song, which was another transatlantic Top 10 hit.

After a two-year layoff between new studio albums (which seemed like an eternity), the Carpenters returned in 1975 with *Horizon*. The platinum album included another hit, the power ballad "Solitaire," and an exquisite version of the 1938 Tommy Dorsey evergreen "I Can Dream, Can't I?" Billy May arranged the track, which was released years before Willie Nelson's *Stardust* and Linda Ronstadt's *What's New* revived interest in standards. Karen and Richard were, as usual, ahead of the game.

Horizon topped the U.K. chart for five weeks, despite stiff competition from Wings' *Venus And Mars* – which had to settle for two weeks on top.

The Carpenters' 1976 album *A Kind Of Hush* spawned Karen's all-time favorite Carpenters single, "I Need To Be In Love." Richard and John Bettis co-wrote the soul-searching ballad with Albert Hammond. Karen teeters between disillusionment and hope on the song, which was the closest thing to "In The Wee Small Hours Of The Morning" in the year of "More, More, More."

The album also included the Carpenters' sprightly version of the '60s pop hit "There's A Kind Of Hush (All Over The World)." The collection went gold in the U.S. and became the Carpenters' fourth album in a row to make the Top 5 in the U.K.

In late 1976, after years of making guest appearances on TV, the Carpenters headlined their first TV special. The music/variety hour, which featured guest stars John Denver and Victor Borge, was a Top 10 hit in the Nielsen ratings. The success of the special led to four other specials over the next four years, on which Karen and Richard played host to such guests as Ella Fitzgerald and Gene Kelly.

In 1977, the Carpenters released their most musically adventurous album, *Passage*. The most memorable track on the album was the space fantasy "Calling Occupants Of Interplanetary Craft." If, at the time, the budget-busting opus came across as a clever stunt, it now seems like a grand pop extravaganza, an inspired blend of madness and majesty. The fun was hearing an act that was usually understated go completely over the top. Richard, a long-time sci-fi fan, teamed with the late Peter Knight to arrange the recording; they were rewarded with a Grammy nomination in early 1978.

Passage spawned two other hits – "All You Get From Love Is A Love Song," an irresistible piece of ear candy that combines traces of big band, dance, and tropical music, and "Sweet, Sweet Smile," a sassy square dance that became a Top 10 country hit.

In 1978, the Carpenters released their classic *Christmas Portrait* album. The collection, which included their 1970 holiday classic, "Merry Christmas Darling," was certified platinum and remains a holiday perennial. Richard conceived and produced the album, striking an ideal balance of sacred and secular, familiar and obscure, cheery and wistful.

In 1979, Karen flew to New York to record an album with Grammy-winning producer Phil Ramone. It was shelved in early 1980, but was finally released in 1996.

Karen and Richard ended a long hiatus in 1981 with the sultry ballad "Touch Me When We're Dancing." The sleek single put the Carpenters back in the Top 20. It also became their 15th #1 adult contemporary hit – which stood as the all-time record until 1997. Also in 1981, Karen and Richard released *Made In America*, their first pop album in nearly four years. The collection featured the lush ballad "I Believe You," the country-tinged "Those Good Old Dreams" and the spunky shuffle "(Want You) Back In My Life Again." The album closed with "Because We Are In Love (The Wedding Song)," which Richard and John Bettis wrote for Karen's 1980 wedding to Tom Burris. The marriage didn't last, but the song has become a wedding favorite.

Karen died on February 4, 1983 at the age of 32. That tragic event marked the end of the Carpenters' career. But the Carpenters music was so full of life, so evocative of both its joy and pain, that even Karen's death hasn't diminished its impact.

Richard's primary focus in the years since Karen's death—besides his growing family—has been on burnishing the Carpenters' legacy. He has personally compiled and annotated numerous anthologies that have been released all over the world, delighting old fans and garnering new ones.

Richard went back to work within weeks of Karen's death. His first project was producing *Voice Of The Heart*, a collection of 10 previously unreleased tracks. Two songs from the album, "Make Believe It's Your First Time" and "Your Baby Doesn't Love You Anymore," became adult contemporary hits. Released that fall, the album was certified gold in the U.S. It did even better in the U.K., where it reached the Top 10.

In 1984, Richard conceived and produced *An Old-Fashioned Christmas*. Richard dedicated the album to Karen, who, he wrote, "was extremely fond of both Christmas and Christmas music." This second holiday album was also certified gold.

The following year, Richard produced *Yesterday Once More*, a double-disk album that brought together many of the Carpenters biggest hits. The collection has been certified double platinum.

In 1987, Richard released his first solo album, *Time,* which featured his own lead vocals on six cuts. Two legendary vocalists also made guest appearances. Dusty Springfield sang the hypnotic ballad "Something In Your Eyes," which became an adult contemporary hit. Dionne Warwick sang "In Love Alone," which Richard co-wrote with John Bettis. Richard composed seven of the 10 songs on the album, including "When Time Was All We Had," which he dedicated to Karen. The song featured a moving flugelhorn solo by Herb Alpert.

Richard also served as a consultant on CBS' *The Karen Carpenter Story.* The TV movie, which received top ratings when it aired on January 1, 1989, introduced a new generation of fans to the Carpenters' music. It also unveiled two exceptional unreleased recordings – "You're The One" and "Where Do I Go From Here?"

Later that year, Richard oversaw the release of *Lovelines.* The album combined six unreleased Carpenters recordings with four tracks from Karen's unreleased solo album.

In 1990, a Carpenters compilation, *Only Yesterday,* topped the U.K. chart for seven weeks. The album dramatized the range of their recorded work, from Hank Williams' "Jambalaya (On The Bayou)" to Klaatu's "Calling Occupants Of Interplanetary Craft."

The following year, Richard produced *From The Top*, a four-CD box set that featured most of the Carpenters hits, as well as a generous sprinkling of previously unreleased tracks and alternate takes.

In 1994, Richard produced *Interpretations*, a collection of Carpenters' versions of songs by other writers. The highlight was a previously unreleased reading of "Tryin' To Get The Feeling Again." Karen and Richard had recorded the song in January 1975, but decided not to include it on the ballad-heavy *Horizon*. The tape was then misplaced – and presumed lost or discarded. Roger Young, the Carpenters' long-time engineer, found the tape in November 1991. In 1994, nearly two decades after he started work on the song, Richard orchestrated the track and completed production.

1994 also saw the publication of Ray Coleman's biography, *The Carpenters: The Untold Story*, for which Richard served as the principal source. That was also the year of the unlikely tribute album, *If I Were A Carpenter*, in which young rock acts saluted the Carpenters. The lineup featured such major names as Sonic Youth, the Cranberries, Sheryl Crow and Dishwalla. Richard lent his moral support to the project and played keyboards on one track – Matthew Sweet's recording of "Let Me Be The One."

In 1997, Richard released his second solo album, *Richard Carpenter: Pianist, Arranger, Composer, Conductor*. The album featured Carpenters classics, along with several new compositions, performed in a brisk baroque style. Amazingly, the album's seemingly exhaustive title doesn't reflect all of the tasks Richard performed at the sessions. He also produced and co-mixed the album and sang background vocals on two of the songs.

That same year saw the release of *Love Songs,* a 20-track compilation of Carpenters classics. The album, which originated in the U.K., rode *Billboard's* pop chart for six months in 1998. Later that year, Richard oversaw the release of *Christmas Collection*, a deluxe two-CD set containing both Christmas albums in their entirety.

In 2000, Richard delivered *The Singles 1969-1981*, an expanded version of the duo's classic greatest hits album.

While Richard has been continuously busy on a professional basis, he's also been extremely active in his personal life. Richard and the former Mary Rudolph were married on May 19, 1984. They are the proud parents of Kristi, Traci, Mindi, Colin and Taylor.

Since 1983, Richard has also settled the affairs of his parents – his dad, Harold, died in 1988, and his mom, Agnes, passed away in 1996.

To unwind, Richard indulges in his other passion – his prized car collection. He specializes in classic American cars – which is fitting for someone who is responsible for so many classic American recordings.

Paul Grein is one of the leading historians in the field of popular music. He interviewed Richard and Karen twice in 1981 (for Billboard *and* The Los Angeles Times) *and has interviewed Richard on several other occasions. He has also written liner notes for several Carpenters compilations, including* The Singles 1969-1981, Interpretations *and* Christmas Collection.

Part One:
We've Only Just Begun

Karen Carpenter:
When I Was 16

By Nancy Hardwick
Star (1973)

Karen Carpenter, the feminine fox in that love-song duo, the Carpenters, is a sexy, outspoken example of a young girl who made up her mind to "make it" in show business, and *did*. Before she was barely 20 years old!

But in spite of all her scrambling to get to the top, Karen is no Women's Libby. In fact, she puts down the hard-nosed bra burners in this interview.

Dressed casually in cutoff Levis, a "Carpenters" T-shirt and furry slippers when I called, I soon discovered that Karen is a very genuine, down-to-earth, foxy lady who makes you feel comfortable to be with. She has a friendly sense of humor, and likes to tell the story of how she and her brother Richard first got their group going, and the obstacles they were up against. Karen also raps about the guys she went steady with in high school – and why she didn't think any of them were worth sacrificing her musical ambitions!

Karen, we're especially interested in rapping with you about your early high school days – what you were like and what got you interested in a show business career?

Well, I looked quite a bit different when I was in high school because I was heavier, about twenty pounds heavier, to tell you the truth. And I was just tired of being fat, so I went on a diet! In fact, just the other day I was cleaning out my bedroom closet, and it was really hard just getting in there. But when I got in, I found this sweater I used to wear in high school. Good Lord, I think I could get into it three times today. I mean I don't know how I ever got through a door. Oh, I really wasn't that heavy, but compared to now… wow!

How long were you on a diet?

Uh, good grief, I think it was five weeks. I had lost like twenty-three pounds. It really worked. It was the water diet… that one where you drink eight glasses of water a day… and I despise water.

Twenty-three pounds? That's incredible. Was it a diet that you yourself designed?

No. I went to a doctor. I decided to go on this diet just at the point when we had our first big hit... and we were running day in and day out. I can remember that we would go to rehearsals and we'd rehearse until about 1 a.m., and then all the guys would want to go to eat at Cocos (and those are the people that make those fantastic onion rings), and I would sit there with my hamburger patty and cottage cheese... while the guys ordered 47-layer cheeseburgers and giant sundaes! I don't know how I did it, because I couldn't do it now.

You were the only girl in the group at that time?

Right. There were five guys, and Richard and I. That was our first group called Spectrum.

Did you have time for guys back then? Did you have a lot of boyfriends? Or one special boyfriend?

When I was in high school I had a couple of boyfriends. But in my junior year, I started getting interested in music and that kind of came in front of everything. But I did have one special guy in my sophomore year, and another one in my junior year.

Were you going steady?

Oh yeah, don't we all? It was a real serious scene. At that point I thought if we ever split up I'd die. You know with the ring, and going steady and all that garbage!

Did you want to marry him?

Oh, sure... that day I did, of course. But when music started to get into my head, kind of everything was, you know, put aside. I mean I dated and everything, but it was kind of hard for guys to understand why music was more important than they were.

What did you tell them?

Well, for example, a guy would ask, 'Do you want to go out Friday night,' and I'd say well, no, we're rehearsing, which didn't go over real big. But that's the way it was. Playing in my brother's group was really all I was interested in. That was when we had the Richard Carpenter Trio. It was a jazz trio. We won the Hollywood Bowl Battle of the Bands in 1966

when I was 16. And that was when we first started trying to get a record contract with our jazz trio, and that was, needless to say, more important than going to the movies with some dumb guy. We were just starting to record at A&M Studios, so I would spend most of my time up there recording. At that point, let's say if we were going to play a job that weekend or whatever, that would always come first.

Did you know that you wanted to go into show business when you were 15 or 16?

When I was about 16, that's when it all happened. That's when the turning point was.

What made you choose show business… what made you decide to follow your ambitions?

Well, Richard has always been musical since the day he was born, and all through his life, his musical interests kind of rubbed off on me, but it didn't hit home until I was 16 years old. And then, all of a sudden, I started to play drums and I started to sing.

Was it mostly your own personal initiative or did your parents or your brother encourage you?

Well, my parents always encouraged us, more so Richard because he is the oldest, but when I decided I was going to get into music, it just sort of happened, mainly because I used to follow Richard when he played a job. Richard and I have always been very close. And when I found out that I could sing and I could play, it seemed a natural thing. And from then on, that's all I was interested in.

What kind of conflicts came up because of your decision to go into music? Were there any conflicts between you and your parents or between you and boyfriends or school?

Well, never between my parents or Richard and myself, because they were always there at all times for whatever was needed. I mean, like they bought all the amplifiers, and if Richard decided we wanted a grand piano, even if we couldn't afford one, which we couldn't at that time, they found a way of getting him one. And when I decided I wanted a drum set, they went and they bought me the best one. My parents have always been like that. If they couldn't afford it at the time, they found a way.

Are you close to your parents today?

Oh, yes, they're right downstairs.

Well, how about any conflicts that might have arose between you and school? You said that you went to college. Did you finish college? Or did your career take precedence over that?

I went through two years of college, and then we signed and that was it. But in college, the choir director influenced Richard and I quite a bit. We met this choir conductor at school, Frank Pooler, who's now our orchestra conductor. Frank is an extremely talented choral man, and when Richard got into the choir in his junior year at school, all of a sudden he developed an interest in vocal (music). That's when he decided on a vocal group. I was just getting started in high school and I had to take gym, which everyone has to take...

How did you like that?

I didn't. I mean, even though I'm very sports-minded, I didn't like running around a football track at 8 o'clock in the morning, freezing to death. So Richard said 'get into the marching band, because if you get in the marching band you get out of gym!' So I said 'great ...what am I going to play?' Richard was real good buddies with the band director because he played gigs with him on the weekends. So he said 'my sister wants to get into the band,' and the band director says 'fine, what does she do?' And Richard says 'nothing'... so he says 'well, okay, I'll give her a glockenspiel,' the bells, or whatever you call it. So I learned how to play that... which isn't really exciting, is it?

But anyway, the bells march in the drum line...because they say it is a percussion instrument, as it were. So I marched in the drum section, and one of my good buddies, Frankie Chavez, who had been playing the drums since he was three years old, was a Buddy Rich freak (you know, Buddy Rich the drummer). He even ate the same food as Buddy Rich! So I used to march down the street playing these stupid bells, watching Frankie play his tail off on the drums. I mean, he really loved it, and all of a sudden I discovered I had an interest in drums. I loved them!

So what happened was I played bells for like two months, and all the time I'm watching Frankie and these other guys play drums, and it soon occurred to me that Frankie was the only one who knew what he was doing. And all of a sudden it hit me that I could play drums as good as nine-tenths of those boys in the drum line... outside of Frankie.

So I told the band director that I wanted to play tenor drum… and he kind of looked at me funny. I finally had to talk him into it, because at that time no girl anywhere was in the drum line of any school in the marching band! So Frankie showed me both drum sticks, what to play, how to play and I became very interested in drums. Before we knew it we were out playing snare drums and we completely reworked the entire drum section. We did like a whole rock and roll number in the drum section. The band couldn't march to it, but it was fun!

But then, before long, I decided I wanted a full set of drums. So Frankie went up and showed me what I should buy… and I bought a brand new set of Ludwigs. And from then on, that was my main interest. At the time, my brother Richard was becoming interested in the vocal thing and we put a vocal group together, and I started to sing at the same time I started to play.

Can you remember some of the first songs you sang?

Oh, wow… we did stuff like "Ebb Tide," and all the stock things at the time like "Yesterday," "Hey Jude." We were all extremely into the Beatles. I guess that's our all time favorite group.

Is it still?

Oh, yeah. Them and the Beach Boys.

Did you break any boy's heart because you put your career before dating?

Well, to tell you the truth, none of the guys I went steady with knocked me out that much that I would have given up or changed what I wanted to do! And I'm so glad that I had enough brains at that point. Because once I finally got into the music thing, and Richard and I started work-ing with the group and all that stuff, nothing seemed to sway what I wanted to do. And, like from the time that we started working, music really became a 24-hour-a-day thing for both of us.

Looking back on your teenage years and your successes, what sort of thoughts would you have for a girl that's about 15, 16 or 17 and wants to be a musician or wants to follow a career in the arts, but she has pressure from her parents or boyfriends?

It depends what the girl wants and if she wants it bad enough. She can figure it out for herself if she's going to stick to it. And if a guy is really in love with her, he would stick with her. I mean, if a guy was really hung-up on a chick… like if a chick wanted to do something really bad, the guy would give of himself and let the chick do what she wants. That's only natural.

How about Karen Carpenter today, are you looking for a guy? How long do you think you'll stay in show business? Do you have any long-range plans?

It's really the only thing that I have an interest for. It's just the love of what we're doing that's really important. And I don't know… there's nobody in particular. There's certain people but not anything that's serious right now. Whether or not I'm looking… I think someone's always looking. When it can happen, I really don't know.

Do you find the role for a woman changing? Do you see more opportunities for a girl to do things that she really wants to do?

Oh yeah! But that's another thing… this bit about Women's Lib. People always call me because they think that being a chick drummer, I'm a Woman's Lib fanatic, and I'm not! Besides, I don't know that much about what they're fighting for. For myself, when I decided what I wanted to do, I went ahead and did it. Nobody got in the way. If they did, you had to figure out a way to get around them. I think anybody who has enough self respect and enough brains can do what they want to do and the bit about blaming it on somebody else is just garbage! There's nobody that's going to stand in the way of somebody if they really want it – male or female! This bit about me being a successful girl drummer… I'm not a successful girl drummer; I'm just a drummer that happens to be a girl that's happy! I have a ball!

Do you like being a star?

Oh yeah, it's a kick. At times it's just a little… well, you have to walk very fast! Sometimes you just want to go out, go down the corner and buy a hamburger. But you really can't do that. That gets me sometimes not being able to walk around on my own! Sometimes you get tired of being protected 24 hours a day but…

And what about your brother, how does he feel about your success?

Oh he loves it. What I'm trying to say is that both of us are extremely happy and it's a great way to live, but it's a 24-hour-a-day job. You're in competition with yourself. But it's really something else to live a life that is not only your own. It's really quite an experience.

What kind of clothes do you like? Do you like clothes?

OH YEAH! Whenever I have a chance I go straight to the clothes stores.

What do you like to wear if you're getting all dressed up – going to a big party or something?

It depends on where I'm going. If it's really formal, it would be a long gown. I like velvets and chiffons and crepes.

Very feminine things?

Yeah, but on the other hand, I love suedes. I have a huge collection of suede. You know, gaucho pants and all that sort of stuff. Suede pants suits and jackets and purses. I'm definitely a suede person.

Your outfits on stage – do you design any of those?

I have a designer whose name is Rick Turner and he works at NBC. He does all the shows like "Carol Burnett" and "Sonny & Cher" and stuff like that. He's very versatile; he can go in many directions. I like my outfits each different from the other. They really have to be or I'd go completely ape.

What style of outfits do you like to wear on stage? I've seen you in long gowns.

Well, I wear long gowns on stage because of playing drums. But what I actually do wear is a gown that's really pants, and when I stand up it looks like a dress. It really works very good. On stage, I can go from a cotton jumper, little puffy tops with a turtle neck (very casual), or to a long chiffon gown, or a low-cut front with a velvet dress with the rest of the dress done in lace.

Sounds like you like very feminine fabrics.

I think it's necessary because when there's seven guys on the stage all in their suits, I like to wear something different from the guys. They all wear the same tux, which is usually coordinated with what I have on. The whole group is coordinated. Let's say I'm wearing red and blue. Richard'll be in red, and the guys will be in blue. Sometimes it takes us weeks to decide what the heck we're going to wear! It's quite involved.

How do you like traveling around with seven guys? What's it like?

Well, in the road group there's 22 people. There's eight of us, a hair-dresser, lighting director, a road manager, five roadies, a manager-manager, a promoter – oh, it's wild! It's like a party.

Are you the only girl?

No, my hairdresser is a girl. Sometimes the guys are able to bring their wives or it depends on whoever's around at the time!

It's like the old chivalrous thing.

Oh, it's really funny to watch the guys on the road – to watch them find the chick they want!

Carpenter groupies?

Oh yeah! They're very clean cut, but they're there! I can be by myself if I want to, but if I need protection there is always someone around. There always has to be. But everybody has such a great time on the road because everybody's really close. And that helps when you're gone five weeks at a time.

Do you enjoy traveling around so much or does it get so hectic you can't really relax?

The last seven to eight months have been relatively easy compared to the way we used to travel. Like a year ago, we used to fly commercial, but there's no way you can carry 22 people and equipment and travel commercially. So about a year and a half ago, we started flying in two Lear jets. And we decided that all of a sudden there were 22 of us (there used to be 14), and we couldn't do it all in two Lears. So now we charter a great big plane, a Cessna 580, and it seats 40. We put everybody in the one big plane, and we have our own flight crew and stewardess. And we just have a ball. I mean we really do. We bowl in the aisles; we have quite a good time.

You have to have a sense of humor…

Oh, we have to, because if we lose control of the show, who will take it? In the oldies medley we have, we have an opening act called "Skiles & Henderson" (who are famous for their noises). And like when we do "Why do the stars go on shining" or "Why do the birds go on singing?" Pete comes out with this gun and he shoots a bird out of the sky and this huge thing falls onto the piano. It's a classic comedy.

It sounds like it's a regular burlesque routine. Who dreams up all this stuff?

We do the medleys, but as for the comedy part, it's up to Bill and Pete. And every night, Bill does something different… he comes out as a robot or whatever. I can never tell what he's going to do next. One night he chases me off the stage, or into the audience, whatever! If I thought about it, I could come up with a story for every night, like kids crawling in the backstage windows when they're not locked and coming right into the dressing room.

Oh yeah? How do you handle that?

You call your manager! But some of the things the kids dream up to get to you are hysterical. They really have some damn good ideas, stuff that I'd never think of. I mean, some kids rent a limousine and follow us into a car or they climb all over the car, or you get into an elevator, they watch to see what floor you get off, and then they just knock on every door on that floor. It's wild!

Karen, we've really had fun talking with you.

I've had fun too. Thanks for calling!

The Carpenters:
They've Only Just Begun…

By Dean Gautschy

TV Radio Mirror **(1971)**

What a super trip! Initially they took a "Ticket To Ride" (the Beatles classic) and the Carpenters, handsome six-foot Richard and his pretty brown-eyed sister Karen, rode nonstop to fame and fortune in the spinning of this 45-rpm disc on airwaves around the world. Their second record release, "Close To You," proved an even bigger hit and the new sound introduced by the pair was sweeping the music industry – the same industry that had previously rejected their talents.

"We were under contract to RCA Victor," recalls Richard with a catlike grin. "But they wanted us to do instrumentals. We cut two records although I told them they would never sell. They were never even released as it turned out. But we don't feel so badly. RCA once rejected Herb Alpert."

Actually, it was Alpert who later became aware of their commercial potential. He flipped when he heard a "homemade" tape of their blended voices, and immediately signed them to a lucrative contract to record for his A&M label. It turned out to be one of the best talent deals the trumpet-playing executive has ever made.

"We've Only Just Begun" was another hit single on their road to success. But the Carpenters are continually bettering their efforts. With the smash success of Oscar-winner "For All We Know," it looks as if they will be around for a very long time, much to everyone's delight.

This summer proved a lot cooler because the Carpenters are such a refreshing welcome to off-season weekly television. Their Tuesday night show on NBC is called "Make Your Own Kind Of Music." The popular Doodletown Pipers and Mark Lindsay, the hip songster, also are regulars on the one-hour musical.

Already the Carpenters' success has been chronicled by music journals such as *Cashbox*. Recently, they were honored by their peers, receiving Grammy Awards as the best new artists and vocal group of 1970. But behind the statistics of record charts and phenomenal sales is a beautiful, warm story of two beautiful and warm people.

The only children of Harold and Agnes Carpenter, Richard and Karen were born in New Haven, Connecticut: Richard on October 15, 1946, and Karen on March 2, 1950. Their father worked for a printing firm. The three-bedroom house in a middle-class neighborhood was small in size but the atmosphere was a loving one.

"Mom has a nice voice," Rich says admiringly, "but she never sang professionally. Dad has a fantastic love for all music. They were very instrumental in helping us get where we are today.

"When I was nine, I started taking piano lessons. The book type of lessons where the teacher comes to your home. I disliked this, and finally convinced my parents they were wasting money. Not until I was about thirteen did I really get into music. This time it was my idea to take lessons again, and by the time I got into high school (Wilbur Cross in New Haven) I was really hooked. In fact, I learned everything the music books could teach me and so I enrolled for more courses at the nearby Yale Music School."

Meantime, Karen played at being Richard's cute kid sister. "I idolized Richard," recalls Karen, "and would tag along with him. You might say I was a tomboy. I loved playing baseball." Rich interrupts with, "It was slightly embarrassing. Karen was a better ballplayer than I was, and when choosing sides for sandlot games, she'd be picked first."

TV Radio Mirror recently interviewed the brother and sister in their suite at the Sands Hotel in Las Vegas. After two weeks singing at the gambling spa, Karen had developed "Vegas throat" (the most common malady singers suffer from in the dryness of the desert).

"It's amazing," Karen says as she clears her sore throat with a cough. "I always figured 'Vegas throat' was some kind of a put-on. But for the past few days I have been losing my voice during the day and luckily finding it before show time."

Both performances each night on a co-bill with comic Don Adams were sold out. Not only is their music pleasant to the ears, but they also give the audience the impression, honestly so, that they are indeed beautiful people.

Barely over 21, Karen in many ways has remained a wholesome sweet sixteen. Not that she's un-hip, either. She's very hip. But she has never lost a youthful innocence, and we hope she never does. All five-feet, four-inches of her frame, from her flowing brown hair to her tiny feet, bubbles with gaiety, although she is very aware of a troubled world.

"The situation of the whole world is a drag," she says. "Everybody fighting everybody. Through our music, Richard and I try to do our best to pull people together — not apart."

Whereas Richard's talent was quite apparent by the time he was in his early teens, Karen didn't test her musical ability until she was in high school: ironically, not as a vocalist, but on the drums. The 120-pounder became a heavyweight drummer without taking a lesson.

When Richard was 16, the Carpenter family was faced with a major decision. For several years Harold Carpenter had been offered another position by a former boss. But it would mean a move to Southern California. By now most everyone in the New Haven area that knew anything about music realized that Rich was destined for bigger things.

"My parents are very hip," Rich smiles. "They didn't have to be told that Los Angeles was where music was happening. So mainly for my future, we moved."

Actually, the Carpenters at first got only a brief glimpse of Los Angeles as they passed through the city and settled off the Santa Ana Freeway in Downey. Harold's job was at the Container Corporation of America in nearby Vernon.

Richard finished his senior year at Downey High School and then enrolled at Long Beach State College. Karen entered South Junior High and soon the Carpenters had adjusted to their new home.

Still Karen was not aware of her musical talents. "Junior high was a waste," she says, "and I didn't do much of anything in music until I was sixteen. This was really the turning point in my career. At Downey High I became a member of the band, but I really couldn't play any instrument.

"It all came about because both Richard and I hated gym. If you took band you didn't have to take gym and run around and do all these weird things. Richard took band and got to know the band director very well.

"When Richard was at Downey High, he marched in and said he wanted to be in the band. They asked him what instrument. He said 'piano,' and they laughed. 'Baby or grand?' Of course everyone knows nobody plays a piano in a marching band, and Richard ended up playing a trumpet, although he knew little about the instrument. But after the band director heard him play the piano, he was so impressed he didn't care if Richard never tooted a note. Sometimes the whole band would just gather around and listen to Richard play.

"So I went to the band director when I was a sophomore – Richard was going to Long Beach State – and I told him I was Richard's kid sister and wanted to be in the band. At first I just was fooling around on the drums and then my parents started to encourage me. They even bought me a set of drums for Christmas. Actually, I taught myself and did most of the things that experienced drummers could do."

The Carpenter kids formed a trio with tuba-bass player Wes Jacobs and started playing sophisticated jazz. Richard did all the arranging and in the summer of 1966, they rehearsed daily from dawn to well into the night.

That same year they entered the Hollywood Bowl Battle of the Bands. Competition was fierce; dozens of other groups were entered. Richard had experience before a live audience. As he says, "My hair was longer and I wore glasses, making me look older, so I was able to pick up club dates while at college."

But little Karen had never been exposed to such a spotlight. She always felt "safe and lost" while performing on a football field with the band. "I thought I'd be scared, but I was too involved in the music to worry about it," she says.

"Well, it was sort of unbelievable," Richard admits. "Karen was the only girl drummer in the contest, and the audience would stare at first in disbelief when she sat down behind the drums… like is this for real? …this pretty little girl behind a massive set of drums.

"When she started playing, though, they believed. She's fantastic. She'd whiz through press rolls, and speedily maneuver the sticks as if she had been born in a drum factory. It was really groovy." The judges thought so, too. For the finale, Wes switched from the bass to the tuba, and the solo, says Richard, "blew everybody's minds." The trio won nine trophies that included the sweepstakes award. An RCA talent scout signed the three to a contract practically before the applause had died down.

"What a letdown," Rich remembers. "I wanted to record some new arrangements, adding vocals to make us sound more commercial. RCA said no, and we cut two jazz numbers, including the tuba solo, that I knew would never sell."

By now the tumultuous sounds of hard rock were sweeping the country. RCA finally realized that Richard was right. The records went unreleased, and RCA decided not to pick up the option on the trio's contract. For a time, the threesome worked local gigs but could not play the big time clubs since Karen was a minor.

Meantime, Karen continued to learn. Following graduation from high school, she joined big brother as music major at Long Beach State. Richard was in the choir. "I thought the group was really groovy," she says, "so I tried out, although I never had done any singing before."

It was the school's choir director, Frank Pooler, who amazed Karen by telling her that she had a good voice. "Mr. Pooler," Karen said admiringly, "is a multi-talented choir genius. We picked up a lot from him."

Later, when Wes Jacobs decided to play classical tuba (he's currently a member of the Detroit Symphony Orchestra), the award-winning trio was "retired." Undaunted, Richard formed Spectrum, a harmony group featuring Karen as lead singer and backed by Cal State pals Leslie Johnston, Danny Woodhams, Gary Sims, and John Bettis.

This time both Richard and Karen felt that their soft-rock sound would make it. Spectrum played such choice dates in the Los Angeles area as the Troubadour, Disneyland, and the Whiskey-A-Go-Go. But they were only a supporting act, and while appearing at the Whiskey, a top hard rock spot, the management became annoyed because the dancers stopped to listen to the Carpenters sing. Apparently the boss figured the club's reputation of presenting only hard rock acts was in jeopardy because he terminated Spectrum's engagement.

"We really hadn't made a dime," says Richard, "and we were very discouraged. We were determined, though… determined to stick it out, but Spectrum gradually broke up."

Around 1966, through their music contacts, the two had met electric bass man Joe Osborn. Joe is originally from Shreveport, Louisiana, and had played in back-up groups for Ricky Nelson, Glen Campbell and many other top recording stars. Joe tinkered around with electronics and began collecting recording equipment he installed in the garage of his home.

More or less as an experiment, Richard and Karen started recording in multi-track, blending their voices into four, six, or more parts by overdubbing as Joe worked the controls at his mini-studio. The resulting tape was aired for several record producers. Each one claimed it would never sell.

Finally, as a last resort, Richard talked his way into A&M Studios and got producer Jack Daugherty to listen. Daugherty was so impressed with the multi-voices he called in Herb Alpert. Soon, under Alpert's personal supervision, the Carpenters cut an album, *Offering*. One of the cuts, "Ticket To Ride," took off as a Top 40 single. Alpert then had the pair record Burt

Bacharach's "Close To You," a song that other singers had recorded with only moderate success. It was used as the title song of the Carpenters' second LP, and became a number one single.

From there the Carpenters started recording hit after hit. The most recent is a ballad by Karen, "Rainy Days And Mondays." Two former members of Spectrum, bassist Dan Woodhams and guitarist Gary Sims, rejoined the Carpenters for the success trip, although Sims is now away on military service. Doug Strawn and Bob Messenger are also group regulars.

Rich and Karen recently bought a modern home for their parents in Downey. Harold Carpenter is retired. His now-famous children continue to live at home – when they're in town, that is. "We haven't had a day off in a year," Karen points out. "Most of the time we've been on the road. But I love living at home – our parents are the greatest."

Neither Karen nor Richard have any steady romantic entanglements. They're both very eligible, although both claim they don't have the time to date very often. Drag racing is their main offstage interest. Richard and a pal own a souped-up Barracuda dragster. "I would like to drive it in competition myself," he says. "I just don't have any spare time."

Someday Karen feels she'll make a good wife for the right man. She digs cooking when she has time, fixing dishes like veal parmesan, eggplant, and a specialty, shrimp salsa. She neither drinks hard liquor nor smokes.

One of the things Richard most admires about his sister is that she has a good head on her shoulders. "Most girls want to get married to the first cat they feel is alright, and sometimes, before they know it, they are divorced. Not Karen. Especially now that she has her career."

Karen agrees with her brother, "As long as we're on the road most of the time, I will never marry. I've seen how marriages have broken up because a wife or husband isn't understanding of the other's career."

Ask Karen what she admires about Richard, she'll tell you, "He has a rich, inborn talent for anything pertaining to music. He's damn good. He's all together."

Richard and Karen launched a new kind of music for the 1970s and the decade is relatively a baby. Yes, the Carpenters have "only just begun" and what a wonderful beginning, too, for such beautiful people.

30

Offering

By Tom Nolan
A&M Compendium (1975)

Editor's Note: Tom Nolan's features and reviews appeared regularly in Rolling Stone, Phonograph Record *and many other publications. Among his best-remembered pieces are* Rolling Stone *cover stories on the Beach Boys and – yes – the Carpenters. This is the first of three excerpts from his essay "The Carpenters: An Appraisal," which was included in the "A&M Compendium" newsletter in 1975.*

Those unfamiliar with the Carpenters' origins might be startled to hear their atypical debut LP, released as *Offering* and later retitled *Ticket To Ride.*

Some of the later elements of the Carpenters' style are present, to be sure – a relatively polished production, Karen's distinctive lead on many tracks, and even a foreshadowing of their subsequent breakthrough single in the lyric of the Richard Carpenter/John Bettis song, "Someday," in which Karen sings the very precognitive phrase "close to you" – but the record is unmistakably a product of the pop rock mainstream of its time.

The a cappella "Invocation," beginning Side One, echoes the choral religiosity of the Beach Boys' "Our Prayer." "Your Wonderful Parade" is prefaced by Richard declaiming a circus barker's sleazy-surrealistic monologue à la Herman Hesse via Joseph Byrd, leader of the art-rocking United States of America. The song itself could have been written by Van Dyke Parks for Harpers Bizarre.

Other influences discernible throughout include the Mamas & Papas, We Five, and early Nilsson. There is restrained use of the then-chic toy, phasing. There are tempo changes, soft but extended jazz-like solos, shimmering Buffalo Springfield-type guitar – and a Buffalo tune, "Nowadays Clancy Can't Even Sing," as well as the folk rock staple, "Get Together."

Offering tends toward being the sort of album many rock critics were encouraging at the time: a post-folk, soft-psychedelic southern Californian mini-oratorio.

31

Moondust And Starlight:
The *Close To You* Album

By John Tobler

By all accounts, Herb Alpert, hitmaking founder of the desperately hip A&M Records, was felt by some (including his employees) to have lost his mind when he persevered with the Carpenters after the desultory chart performance of *Offering,* the duo's debut album. His staff may have thought he was hanging around too much with Gram Parsons of The Flying Burrito Brothers, who wore Nudie suits with embroidered designs of tablets and drug paraphernalia.

In fact, what apparently happened was that Alpert had just heard Richard and Karen's newly-recorded cover version of "Close To You," a Burt Bacharach/ Hal David composition which had previously been recorded by Dionne Warwick, but had only been the B-side of a minor hit. In fact, the original recording of the song was released as the B-side of a 1963 US Top 50 hit by Richard "Dr. Kildare" Chamberlain titled "Blue Guitar." (Incidentally, both the Chamberlain and Warwick versions listed the song's title as "They Long To Be Close To You," while the Carpenters' rendition put the first four words in parentheses.)

Alpert played the Carpenters' recording to Bacharach over the phone, and Bacharach loved it, although it was arranged quite differently from Warwick's 1965 reading. Released as a single, it became the first number one hit for the Carpenters, as well as the title track of their second album.

The title track wasn't the only huge hit single on the *Close To You* album. Almost as massive was the enduring and romantic "We've Only Just Begun," written by Paul Williams and Roger Nichols, which became their second million seller in three months. This song had started life as a TV commercial for the Crocker Citizens Bank of California, and its tunefully romantic sentiments captivated Richard Carpenter when he heard the brief commercial. Richard asked if there was a complete song (which, at the time, there wasn't), but fortunately, Williams and Nichols were staff writers at A&M Records, to which the Carpenters were also signed, so matters were easily resolved.

Williams & Nichols also wrote "I Kept On Loving You," which appeared on the album, as well as being the B-side of the "Close To You" single.

There were a number of other above-average tracks on *Close To You,* including the duo's second Beatles cover. *Offering* had featured "Ticket To Ride," while *Close To You* included "Help!" Similarly, just as *Offering* had included covers of two folk rock standards (the Youngblood's "Let's Get Together" and Buffalo Springfield's "Nowadays Clancy Can't Even Sing"), *Close To You* featured a cover of Tim Hardin's "Reason To Believe." In addition, *Close To You* contained two more Bacharach songs in "Baby It's You" (a hit for The Shirelles which was also covered by The Beatles), and the under-rated "I'll Never Fall In Love Again" (originally by Dionne Warwick, but a bigger hit in the UK for Bobbie Gentry).

Where *Offering* had included a preponderance of original material written by Richard Carpenter (with lyrics by John Bettis), this time there were only four such songs, all dating from the pre-fame period when Richard, Karen and Bettis were members of Spectrum, a close harmony group. In comparison with their later efforts (such as "Goodbye To Love," "Top Of The World," etc.), the Carpenter/Bettis songs here are mostly of minor significance. The exception is "Mr. Guder," which was written about a supervisor at Disneyland, whom Richard and Bettis (who once worked there as a musical duo) found officious. This song was featured in the Carpenters' live shows during the early 70s, and it possesses a curious non-mainstream appeal.

Also of note on *Close To You* is the delightfully bouncy "Love Is Surrender," an "outside" song (penned by Ralph Carmichael) which must rank as one of the great undiscovered gems of the Carpenters' recorded catalog.

Overall, *Close To You* was a huge step forward from *Offering,* and it became the first of a succession of gold albums for the Carpenters. It included two signature songs ("We've Only Just Begun" and the title track), which the siblings almost certainly felt obliged to perform at every subsequent live show until Karen's tragically early death. Many years later, this album remains one of the duo's finest achievements, and in many ways, it became the blueprint for subsequent collections.

John Tobler is the author of The Complete Guide To The Music Of The Carpenters.

The Grumbling Began:
The Carpenters As The Enemy?

By Tom Nolan

A&M Compendium (1975)

With their first two hits, "Close To You" and "We've Only Just Begun," the Carpenters simultaneously attracted the concentrated affection of their newfound fans and the hostility of another segment that distrusted them from first hearing. They were both loved and hated from the very moment they were noticed at all. Why?

American popular music has always reflected the aspirations and intended identities of its listeners. The mothers and fathers of rock criticism in the sixties "discovered" that fans were buying more than music – they were purchasing lifestyles. But it was ever thus: Okies paid for Hank Williams' beatific moonstruck grin as well as for his 78s. Swing nuts must have made some connection between Krupa's goofy gum chewing and those crazy drum choruses; his *attitude* was as attractive as his art.

So here are these neatly-dressed kids, a polite-seeming brother and sister team, materializing like a weird hallucination in the midst of acid rock and offering their alternative to "In-A-Gadda-Da-Vida," singing, of all things, a *bank commercial*. The grumbling began, and grew louder in proportion with their success. You'd think they were an arm of the government, the way some people reacted!

What was it they thought the Carpenters represented? Domesticity, perhaps? The nuclear family? Saturdays spent shopping for sofas at Sears? Capitalism itself? There were those so turned off by what they thought they detected beneath the music that they spoke of the Carpenters as the enemy.

The enemy. Imagine. Poor Karen and Richard! Just trying to make their music. All this rancor…

The Carpenters
And The Creeps

By **Lester Bangs**
Rolling Stone (1971)

Where there's lots of money being made, as any hack journalist will tell you, there's probably some kind of story; and when a once-floundering group has two giant hits in a row, some psychological transaction must be taking place between them and the public. Success stories like Melanie and Grand Funk are obvious; but what about a group like the Carpenters, who are at present riding high even though they don't seem to have any particular image, concept, much material or anything definite except a pleasant-voiced girl and a facile arranger? Is there some subtle catalytic ingredient hiding somewhat beneath that too-clear surface? Or is their whole phenomenon just blind coincidence?

Thus it was that I took my musical sensibilities in my hands and attended a Carpenters concert. Oh, I had really liked "We've Only Just Begun." (I'd just re-fallen in love with a childhood sweetheart at the time it was riding the radio, and it was, well, it was Our Song.) Even if it did originate in a bank commercial. Karen Carpenter had a full, warm voice, and her brother Richard's musical settings were deft and to the point. The LP cover and promo pix showed 'em side by side, identical, interchangeable boy-girl faces grinning out at you with all the cheery innocence of some years-past dream of California youth. Almost like a better-scrubbed reincarnation of Sonny & Cher.

What also sparked my curiosity was the question of audience: who pays five bucks for a Carpenters concert? Somehow you couldn't see the usual rock show crowd of army-fatigued truckers and seconaled stooges. But they must have found a major following *somewhere* because, in San Diego at least, the show was totally sold out.

We got there late and, indeed, the first thing you noticed was the audience – and what was striking was its diversity: little tots, Bobby Sherman nymphets, college couples (rather sedately straight for the most part), Mom and Pop and a smattering of grandparents. And all of them sitting there

37

open-mouthed, staring solemnly at the stage where a rather delicate looking fellow named Jake Holmes was hunching his shoulders intensely and singing in a broken near-whisper a song about alienation and "people whose elbows touch but never their eyes."

The crowd flipped for Holmes, brought him back for an encore, and then we all settled back to pleasant anticipation of what the Carpenters, minor mystery that they were, could have for a stage act. But nothing – *nothing* that we might have ever dreamed of could have prepared us for what we saw when those curtains parted.

In the first place, there is no balance, no center of attention. Here are six people on a stage singing and playing various instruments, and your eye just keeps shifting from one to another without ever finding a nexus to focus on. They are an odd and disjunct congregation. My girl said they made her nervous; I would say that they have the most disconcerting collective stage presence of any band I have ever seen.

Besides being a motley crew, they are individually peculiar looking. Here it almost becomes cruel to go on, but there is no getting around it, especially since most of the music was so bland, and their demeanor so remarkable that you could spend the entire concert wondering at the latter without once getting bored. I found the Band almost like tintypes of themselves, and Van Morrison, so visually static himself, had me laid back dreaming; but I couldn't take my eyes off the Carpenters. I'll never again be able to hear "We've Only Just Begun" without thinking, not of a sentimental autumn as I used to, but inevitably of that disgruntled collection of faces.

The first thing is that Karen Carpenter not only sings lead but also plays drums – she's pretty damn good, too, seldom falters – but singing from behind that massive set she just doesn't give you much to look at, lovely and outgoing as she is. This band should invest in a drummer.

Brother Richard plays piano, and he's excellent technically, if not emotionally, ripping out crisp though somewhat stereotyped demi-jazz lines that even managed to save an otherwise awkward version of "Nowadays Clancy Can't Even Sing." But watching him… he was a chubby, rather nervous little fellow with a round face, pudding-bowl hair and a white suit with vast lapels that only served to accentuate that odd combination of qualities, giving him a strong resemblance to the cloven-hoofed conductor of a barnyard symphony in an old cartoon. And in quiet numbers, when the lighting was subdued and he was tinkling out pearly arpeggios, he would stare up and off into space with mournful, almost-crossed eyes, as passionate as Chopin in the throes of creation.

The others, guitarist Gary Sims and Doug Strawn, who plays electric clarinet and tambourine and sings a couple of numbers in a fine voice that they should utilize more (the promo sheet says he's "a former barbershop quartetist"), are pretty ordinary looking cats. Bassist Bob Messenger, who doubles on tenor sax and flute, looks vaguely like a Walt Kelley caricature of Joe McCarthy as a badger (it says here, "When not playing good music for the Carpenters, his job is to keep the kids out of trouble – he's the oldest member of the band"), and Danny Woodhams, who does backup vocals and plays tambourine and "assorted junk," as Richard said, is absolutely incredible. He looks about like your average bushy-headed LA Whisky scene-maker, with his Edwardian velour jacket and Maltese Cross earring, but he is the most outrageous ham I've ever seen in a professional group. Maybe it's because he doesn't really *have* anything to do but sing once in awhile and bash the tambourine with all the pyrotechnic intensity of an Elvin Jones.

The music itself was entirely predictable, a pleasant and mildly bracing flow: ice cream music. Their few originals, like "Mr. Guder" (cute moralizing about a tight-assed Disneyland boss) are never going to be their hits, and, like their albums, their show depends on bright, cream-puffy arrangements of 1965 Beatles songs, old Burt Bacharach hits, and innocuous "hip" standards like "Reason To Believe" and "Get Together."

Strawn sang a couple of rather weird ragtime/hoedown "novelty" numbers, with lyrics like "There went Grandma swingin' on the outhouse door" and breaks right in the middle for short spoken "Laugh-In" tradeoffs between band members. They also did one bit where Strawn asked for a volunteer from the audience for a "magic trick," selected a little girl from the first row and when he got her on stage he asked how old she was. "Seventeen." The girl, naturally, is giggling and blushing and Strawn does a broad double take when she tells her age and makes her stand a few inches away. Howls from the audience. Now he closes his eyes and says that she should think of a number and he will guess it. "Go ahead," he says, "pick a number – any number between three and five!" Dynamite. Strawn sends the girl back to her seat and they're off into another old Dionne Warwick hit.

As we oozed out of the theater I looked around me and speculated that this must have been a sort of diplomatic project in many homes: Mom and Dad would come and learn to dig the kids' music. I was still dazed from the absolute incongruity of those faces, and I *had* to ask some of the people around me what they'd thought. I really wanted to ask them what in the hell had ever brought them to this oddball event in the first place, but a lot of them looked pretty odd themselves, in a self-consciously middle-class sort of way, so I just turned towards a well-dressed, rather cold looking blonde girl about 20 and said: "I'm doing a piece on this show for a magazine. What'd you think of it?" She just stood there staring at me in an incredulous, slightly hostile way: "What?" I repeated myself, and still she stood there and just stared at me, her mouth open, her boyfriend behind her eyeing me suspiciously. They simply could not believe that someone could be asking such a thing of them. They looked as if I were insane, or had sidled and asked for a handout. And me with a suit on and everything! I gave up. We glumly found the way to our car and got in feeling curiously numb, just as the whole evening had been mildly unsettling on some peculiar level. I was not acclimated only to longhaired audiences, but something about band and audience both at this one just gave me the creeps. All around us on the tiers of the 11-story parking lot, kids were gunning their engines, screeching out, laying rubber. I reflected that you seldom heard that when the cars were filled with stoners leaving rock concerts; but what that and all the rest ultimately signified I never will fathom.

On The Road With The Carpenters

By Digby Diehl
TV Guide (1971)

Editor's Note: Digby Diehl interviewed the Carpenters three or four times over a period of a month in 1971. His work on this TV Guide *feature led to an invitation from the duo's manager, Sherwin Bash, to write a stage act for the Carpenters, who would soon be appearing in Las Vegas for the first time. Accompanying Karen and Richard on tour that summer, Diehl was informed by Bash (in no uncertain terms) that his "real job" was to get Karen out from behind the drums. It wasn't an easy assignment, but within several months, she hesitantly drifted toward center stage and the Carpenters hired another drummer. Although Karen became a confident front for the group, Diehl recalls that Richard remained rigid and uptight on stage: "I never got him out from behind the piano."*

When you're on tour, the whole world looks Motel Green. The Cincinnati motel room that houses Richard Carpenter, one half of the hot new singing team that has dared to put romance back into pop, is no exception. The sun beats down at a muggy, unrelenting 90 degrees. The air conditioner is stuck on fast-freeze. The ever-present TV set, its big eye blank now, stares out over a roomful of depressing furniture and obscenely oversized beds.

Richard sips iced tea and takes a tranquilizer. His sister Karen just grouses. They are feeling travel-worn, homesick and apprehensive about tonight's concert, one of 15 one-nighters in the last three weeks.

The motel-green telephone rings and Richard trips over his half-opened suitcase to grab it. This time it is not an irate conductor in Minneapolis or a booking agent in Kansas City; it's Agnes, the *original* Carpenter, calling from the family home in Downey, California. Only the news is not sunshine. Her voice crackles over the phone. Ma Carpenter is giving her now-famous offspring a motherly piece of her mind.

Richard wilts into the motel-green bedspread as Ma Carpenter reads an angry letter from a fan who had brought her family to a concert in Hershey, Pennsylvania, last week and was dismayed that the Carpenters did not sign autographs after the show. Richard is sputtering, "But Mom… but Mom…" What Mom doesn't know is that it was pouring rain in Hershey, a thousand kids were about to rush the car, and they're lucky they weren't run over. Karen is just plain furious: "We're practically the only group in America that signs autographs, and we nearly get killed every time we do it."

Minutes later, an anguished and dutiful Richard is calling Hershey, apologizing and promising to send autographed copies of the three Carpenters albums. The woman, only slightly mollified, lays it right out there. "Richard," she says, "we were very disappointed with you in Hershey." Karen is wild: "This is incredible! Could you just see Mick Jagger apologizing for not giving an autograph?"

In fact, there's probably no one else in the whole hard-nosed world of pop music who would have made that phone call except the Carpenters. But it is this honest, eager-to-please folksiness that separates the Carpenters from the Jaggers. They want everybody to love them. It is their richly harmonied, romantic music that makes them as sweetly unique in the world of rock as *Love Story* in the world of contemporary literature. Arriving just last year in the Top 10 with "Close To You" and "We've Only Just Begun," the Carpenters have already collected Grammy Awards as the best new artists and for the best contemporary performance by a vocal group of 1970. Their success has also won them another kind of accolade: their own summer TV show, "Make Your Own Kind Of Music."

The telephone call over, the Carpenters manage to get it together, hop in a rented car and head for the bowling alley. As we walk in, a few of the Ohio Mayflower set give Richard's long Prince Valiant haircut a hostile look. Karen laughs, "Why don't they understand that we're just two kids from Downey who like to take showers?"

We settle down in Alley 19 and the kids start chuckling. Also talking. To hear them tell it, life is one long series of comic chases through motel corridors, practical jokes, and the general stuff of a college spree amongst the entourage of 15 musicians and equipment. In Lansing, Michigan, for instance, the horseplay climaxed in a dressing room water balloon fight that left the entire group soaking wet minutes before curtain time.

Here in Cincinnati, the game has been to elude three teenage girls who have been following them cross-country ever since they played Carnegie Hall a week previously. Richard, hardly a lady-killer, is befuddled by the relentless fans: "Everybody else in the music business meets a chick for one night and she's happy, they're happy. But me, I've got this whole troop that won't go home. What am I supposed to do?"

Unlike many of their middle-America counterparts, Karen and Richard are so immersed in their music that they are socially and politically uninvolved. "Sure, we think the world's a big mess," says Richard, laying down a sharply breaking hook. "But we couldn't get seriously into politics now because we're too busy."

It may be part of the secret of the Carpenters' success that many listeners are taking refuge in nostalgia for better days gone by, love stories and love songs. "For the kids to make number one records with their romantic sound, when the rest of the music scene is still heavy rock, amazes even me," Sherwin Bash, their unflappable veteran manager, told me later. "A song like 'Rainy Days And Mondays' is the kind of thing Sinatra might have done when he was doing songs like 'Violets For Your Furs'! It's instant nostalgia. The Carpenters' music may never be put in a time capsule, but the people certainly love it now. There's a young pretty girl and a young bright-eyed boy doing pretty things they love and that's all we're talking about."

Perhaps the basic Carpenter appeal *is* this simple, but their musical development was anything but. It began with Richard's obsessive love of music that made him a jazz-piano whiz at 16. As a high school student growing up in New Haven, Conn., he studied the classics at the Yale School of Music during the day and was playing with jazz groups at night. "But all the time, I was listening to pop music," he recalls. "My three B's were the Beatles, Bacharach and the Beach Boys." When the family moved to Downey, Richard formed his own musical group and began writing and arranging his own songs.

Starting out with a set of chopsticks and four bar stools, Karen paradiddled along with records at home and proved to be almost as natural a musical talent as Richard. When he heard her keeping up with the complex polyrhythms of Dave Brubeck's *Time Further Out*, weaving through 11/4, 9/8 and 5/4 time with ease, Richard joined her campaign to get a set of drums. Within weeks, she played with her brother for a local production of *Guys And Dolls* and became a regular member of his jazz trio, along with a young bass and tuba player named Wes Jacobs.

A year later, they entered the Hollywood Bowl Battle Of The Bands, a musical competition open to amateurs under the age of 21, and swept the field. They earned the highest score ever recorded in the contest. Richard won Outstanding Instrumentalist, the group won First Place Combo, and they took the sweepstakes prize for Best Group of the Evening. Immediately, they were signed to a recording contract by RCA.

Their enthusiastic producer saw in the Carpenters the vanguard of a new sound: rock tuba. To no one's surprise, rock tuba did not turn out to be the new sound. Wes Jacobs became disgusted with the pop scene and took his tuba to the Detroit Symphony Orchestra. Karen and Richard retrenched with a new musical group and began two years of beating on record company doors.

"We formed a harmony vocal group called Spectrum with some guys that were in the choir with us at Long Beach State College," Richard is saying. "We used to play the Hoot Night at The Troubadour every Monday, just for the chance of being heard by someone for 15 minutes. Wow, if you think we look square now, you should have seen us with our crewcuts and blue-velvet jackets."

Richard cheerfully admits his group sounded a bit like Muzak when following some of the rock sound machines they played with, like Steppenwolf. "But the kids liked our sound. Our big break was a date at the Whisky-A-Go Go in Hollywood, where the kids all sat and listened and dug us. Well, at the Whisky, if no one's dancing, the management figures something's wrong. The owner threw us out and the group broke up shortly after that."

The breakup of Spectrum turned out to be a lucky break. Left with only their two voices, Richard and Karen created harmonies by blending with themselves on multitrack tapes. "Wow, we couldn't believe the results," says Karen. "All of a sudden this ten-ton thing was born. This couldn't miss!"

A&M Records producer Jack Daugherty agreed and took their tapes to Herb Alpert, who signed the Carpenters immediately. They ran up a bill for $47,000 on a first album that made no impressive sales dent. Herb's confidence never wavered, and one day he played a Bacharach-David song for them that Dionne Warwick had recorded without particular success. The song was "Close To You."

Shortly thereafter, Richard, with a remarkable ear for pop hits, heard a Crocker Citizens Bank commercial aimed at young newlyweds who had "only just begun" to borrow. They recorded "We've Only Just Begun" and it flew to the top of the charts. Since then, the Carpenters have had just one long musical blaze of success.

"The television show is very exciting for us," says Karen, "but introductions and comedy bits aren't really our thing; basically we're musicians. Richard would like to experiment more with musical innovations eventually."

"There's so much you can do with the voice that I don't think would be commercially cool to do just yet," he says. "I'd like to do a choral album like that vocal segment of *2001*, tone clusters and radical harmonics."

But it's time to go. Richard underlines his point by throwing three straight strikes and, in high spirits, heads the rental car toward the Cincinnati Gardens.

The concert is a plague. They've been booked into this hockey rink where the stage is too high and there is a seven-second echo delay bouncing off the walls. Promotion has been weak, the dressing room smells of old ice skates, and everyone is feeling low. But it's all part of life on the road. Once on stage, the Carpenters start singing, and suddenly that hockey rink is the most romantic place in the world. Afterwards, they sign autographs, just like Mom told 'em.

Digby Diehl, Los Angeles-based arts critic, wrote the liner notes for several Carpenters albums, including The Singles 1969-1973. *He is a literary correspondent for "Good Morning America," and has written several non-fiction books.*

Concert Review:
Sands, Las Vegas,
March 24, 1971

Variety (1971)

The turn to mellowness in pop tunes and presentation was given a tremendous boost by Karen and Richard Carpenter in their immensely successful second album, *Close To You*. What makes the pair even more intriguing is the exact sound recreated for bounds outside of a recording studio. Banks of electronic gear, extra speakers spaced about the room, and a precise balance bring the spinning disk to life. Richard, at the electric piano, handles all the narrative well, coloring the group as "a road version of the Partridge Family." Karen, ensconced behind a battery of drums, manages to be seen very often and heard to very good advantage, her clear voice calmly picking its graceful way among the lyrics.

A couple of doubtful inclusions are a Christmas song and a rather pointless and callow break in the song action when musician Doug Strawn brings up a girl from the audience for a nothing five minutes or so. Otherwise the logging is very good, ranging from their very best known lacquerings to novelties such as a raucous throwback to the 1920s and a Mason Williams antic tune.

Helping to achieve the Carpenter blend are sidearm Strawn on reeds and rhythm noisemakers; Bob Messenger, electric bass, tenor sax and flute; Gary Sims, electric bass and guitar, and Danny Woodhams, electric bass.

Rainy Days And Carpenters Always Get Me Down

By Ken Michaels
Chicago Tribune Magazine (1971)

Where *are* they? Are they here? Wait – here they come now. Outside, everybody. Hurry up! The *kids* are here! A red Maserati zooms off La Brea, dips under the 8-by-24-foot "CARPENTERS" sign, zips through the tunnel entrance of Charlie Chaplin's old studio, past the obsequious guard, and scoots into a parking slot stenciled "Daugherty."

Casually, out of the Maserati climbs one of the kids, Karen, blasé about the whole world, looking like an unhappy Jane Wyman. Her Act: custom-job Maserati, sunglasses atop the hair like songwriter Burt Bacharach wears his, sloppy saffron sweater drooping over slacks. Go in, get this act over and get on to the next.

From the Maserati's driver's side tumbles the other kid, Richard, his all-American shoulders tossing under a worried, boyish face. Big hard workday coming up. Where *is* everybody?

The sound stage is like a junior high school gym. Basketball court with boards and hoops overhead, vari-colored streamers and pompons. Bleachers filled with boppers.

An orchestra, a chorus, four supporting singers and musicians, and in the center the kids themselves: Richard at the Electrapiano Rock-si-Chord, Karen at drums, holding a mike. Bored. Been thru this a jillion times. Let's get on with it, what do you say, hey?

Karen's a good singer. She knows what she's doing, what the market wants. Soft rock, they call it. Low-key stuff with wide appeal. For a while, as she sings "For All We Know," the Oscar-winning song from *Lovers And Other Strangers*, Karen makes us *believe* it. She feels it, the sound system issues it superbly, everything is right. A mood is created; everybody forgets every-thing except the singer and the song. But then – between phrases – Karen drinks from a paper cup, yawns ho-hum, is this putting me to sleep. She frowns at another phrase, sticks her tongue out at it. Done it so many times it's a drag.

When the ensemble does Richard's composition "Benediction," Richard's blue eyes keep asking where the hell did they get this chorus from? And this director? Every bar or so Richard leaps from his stool to the orchestra and chorus and makes them stop. "Nope. Not right. Like *this*." He takes over from the director, hisses "shhhh" to violins, shoots a dirty look toward the brass section. The chorus? Forget it.

Everybody's talking. Talking when Richard solos on Electrapiano Rock-si-Chord, talking when Karen sings. Producer-talk, manager-talk, agent-talk, PR man-talk, gopher-talk, bopper-talk. And everybody has his own camera: director, orchestra members, chorus, the bleacher kids. Everybody is taking everybody's picture. It's an Instamatic orgy.

During the break, the whole cast does the break act. Take five, gang. Exaggeratedly they stagger from the studio, wilted. Whew! The heat! Where're the *Cokes*? Too much! Whew! Outasight!

"You can meet them now," a publicist whispers. "Just for a minute though, they said." From a dull passage the kids emerge, with downer faces. Don't feel like the greeting bit again. Uptight today. Led by the publicist, Richard bounds over, dumps the annoyance look, spreads a capped smile, offers a strong handshake and says, "Hi, how are you, nice to see you." Then he darts past to the Maserati.

As Karen approaches, her frown deepens. You touch her hand hello and she frowns more, then smiles while she's frowning and says, "Glad to meet you." She goes silent, looking trapped. Disgusted that she had to come out here at all.

What do you break ice with?

You tell Karen you notice she's working with a big chorus today.

"We've worked with choruses before."

Nice full orchestra, too. Where are they from, anyway?

"Have no idea." Karen tosses a hand. "All I know is they send us the best. They get the best singers and best musicians and send them to us." Karen leans tight against the bricks, maintains the frown. She's 21.

The publicist presses in, "The minute is up," he grins sheepishly at Karen. "Good," she says, and stalks away. At the Maserati the boppers take her picture. Karen smile-frowns for them.

"Big day today," says the publicist. "Lot of pressure. They got the Bowl tonight. It'll be their largest appearance ever. Maybe catch them this aft during Bowl rehearsal, talk then. Good dealie-doo?"

Meet the Carpenters — A&M Records' young brother-sister hit-makers whose gentle harmony, wholesome image and natural, unpretentious personalities have virtually crashed through to make them the nation's number one recording team. Their sonorous magic has endeared them to music fans of every age and taste, and may be marking the beginning of a new musical mood for the '70s, bringing back the three H's — hope, happiness, harmony. With soft-pedaled persistence and talent galore, these melodic siblings have revolutionized the music industry.

A&M Records Publicity Sheet

"You meet Jack Daugherty? He discovered them. Was working at North American Aviation, see – a regular job. One night he heard the kids' tape, took them to Herb Alpert, who flipped. Jack Daugherty's their producer now, has a big office at A&M Records, has nothing to worry about. Meet him at the Bowl. If not, get talking to him at the cocktail party Stanley Kramer's throwing afterward. You can talk with the kids then, too. Good dealie-doo?"

Afternoon at Hollywood Bowl. Where *are* they? Are they here? From between massive pillars you look out and up forever past green-canvassed box seats and hundreds of rows of brown chairs to the top, to the sky, where benches and seats up there under the trees look like doll-house furniture. Enough to scare the hell out of any performer.

"How many expected tonight?"

"We'll fill it. Over 16,000. Lots of folks, and..." the agent rubs together money thumb and fingers "...lots of money."

A roar of Maserati in the lot, clomp upstairs, a squeeze between pillars, and the kids trot casually to stage center.

One number later, Richard sweats at the Electrapiano Rock-si-Chord. A gopher dashes to him with Coke. Richard guzzles, blows whew, wipes his sweat-wet hair, rips off his polo shirt.

Mike in hand, Karen slumps, buried in the drum set. "*Wah*" mouths Karen into her mike, testing sound. And the "*Wah*" booms out over 10 acres.

Doing "Ticket To Ride," they get in trouble. Richard stops the sound. "Not right. Too boxy. Unbalanced." A bearded engineer hotfoots it backstage to bawl the hell out of an assistant. Richard says, "Start." A second later he orders, "Stop." He shakes his head: "Still not it. Less, Danny, more Karen." Assistants fly, adjust the eight front mikes and five back. You wonder why the kids couldn't skip the rehearsal and lip synch the program.

51

Trouble breaks during "Do You Know The Way To San Jose?" "More bottom. Terribly boxy. More Karen." Richard hops on the stool, pounds the Electrapiano Rock-si-Chord. His drawers keep drooping, he keeps yanking them up. His body is wet and red. He shouts damn and hell. He swigs voraciously. Looks for hope from Daugherty, high in the control booth. Daugherty's face is gray. Daugherty says nothing. Karen says, "*Wah.*"

"She's really nice – and loves how I do her hair. She sits back in the chair and hums all the pop songs." Karen's hairdresser – in her twenties but looking like a bopper – perches at the reflector pool by the stage apron. "Karen never thought she could sing. All through high school she wanted to, but couldn't. One day somebody told her to sing everything an octave lower. She did and it was like a fairytale. It was beautiful. Isn't her hair nice? It's nice to work with, too."

The orchestra is rushing things. The director's hair is funny, uptight. The choir's voices are gone – no matter how many mikes they can't be heard past the apron – except for one frog in the bass section whom Richard keeps trying to find in his constant trips to the podium, so he can kick the guy out. Richard looks familiarly at Karen: Geez, if I could only find Frog-voice, if I could only run this myself, get rid of all these cretins, get it right! Karen nods familiarly: I know what you mean.

Wah. Boxy. Crap. Hell. *Wah.*

They wrap it up. Daugherty and Richard have a summit meeting among scattered music stands. Karen feigns exhaustion: Whew! Too much! Agents and gophers scamper to her rescue, to hug and soothe, to whisper Hollywood nothings in Karen's ear. "Bad time to talk to them now," the publicist says. "You can catch them tonight."

> *Hi, everybody, we're the Carpenters. It's really great to be in _____, and it's great to be listening to _____ [D.J.], one of the hippest music masters on the air. We're glad you're tuned in... and we hope you drop in at the _____, where we'll be playing until _____. It'd be really great to see you all in person.*
>
> A&M Records Radio Spot Sheet

Hollywood at night: Where *are* they? Are they here? A lousy rock group with two drummers yeah-yeahing each other to death is trying to turn the crowd on. Not 16, but 18,000 tonight. It's SRO at $7.50 top. Boppers, Mom and Dad, Uncle Ray and Aunt Flossie, all nice and clean and pressed.

Down front in boxes sit 42 members of the Carpenter clan. Mom Carpenter, in pink, is up and around, making pantomime greetings as the amplifiers scream and the drummers freak, go native on the stage.

Then a 45-minute sound setup, electricians all over the place. Then a rustling of granny dress, and from behind the Samson pillars – backed by dawn-pink afterglow – lilt two silhouettes: one moving to the silhouetted Electrapiano Rock-si-Chord, the other to silhouetted drums. Sidemen take places by silhouetted mikes, violin bow silhouettes are poised. A downbeat, a drum roll: LADIES AND GENTLEMEN – THE CARPENTERS!

The boppers freak. Richard smiles. The sidemen smile. Karen smiles. It's total metamorphosis. No slumping, no glumness tonight. As Karen sings she toddles like a bopper, rolls her eyes like dolly. Wonderful! How did we ever make it so quickly to the top? Hollywood Bowl sellout? Don't ask me. I can't believe it, either, but here we are!

The music is pretty eclectic: pop and rock, surf and jazz, Bacharach, Beatles and Beach Boys. They do "Help" and "Superstar" and "Baby, It's You." Finishing a Bacharach medley with "Do You Know The Way To San Jose?" they rush to a snap-off ending with computer-like precision. The crowd goes ape. Karen wipes mock-sweat from mock-brow: Wow! She rolls dolly eyes: Ooooogh! Whew! Hard song? How did we ever get through it without flaw? Whew! Boy!

Richard shouts "Hi" to the kids in the trees. He gets a roaring "Hi" back. He tells how just a year ago, before they made it big with "Ticket To Ride" and "Close To You" he and Karen were just like you guys up there, sitting up there in the cheap seats, too. And now look at us. Eighteen thousand people, and *we're* down here! Is that beautiful?

Richard plays one of his compositions, then tells the audience about the latest gold album, *Carpenters*, and about an appearance on an upcoming TV show, and about how Stanley Kramer personally called them up to do the soundtrack for his movie *Bless The Beasts And Children*. They play the soundtrack number, then Karen talks to the audience about the career, introduces Herb Alpert Tijuana Brass, who smiles and nods out in the 10th row. Then the group does two more songs which sound like the last ones they did.

The audience response is polite applause. They clap more at the beginnings, like a contest: Who can recognize the song first? That's all that seems to matter.

With a tiny spotlight on her face, Karen – not quite like Judy Garland – tiptoes to the apron and whispers how swell it is to be up from those humble beginnings, how she and Richard walked the streets of L.A. with only that little tape recording in their pocket, how they'd like to say to you people out there a simple – "thanks."

When Karen finishes, the Carpenters bow offstage and the audience – politely applauding – starts getting up to leave. It's an embarrassment. Will the Carpenters be allowed to stay off? Won't they be brought back?

From nowhere they reappear, sprinting forward like middle-distance runners, bowing profusely. The audience sits, claps to a mild plateau, then cools it fast. The Carpenters run backstage, pivot, and like fire-horses race on again, bowing. The audience sits down. Then they get up. Then they sit down again. The audience doesn't know what to do.

What's the matter with you people, don't you know *talent?* With *that* kind of angry face, who rises from an apronside box, clapping her curls off? Karen's hairdresser. Like a shill she's up tall, pounding her palms together, her curls jumping like Shirley Temple's, giving filthy, resentful looks to anybody who dares remain seated, which is everybody.

But the hairdresser accomplishes Mission Impossible. First the familial cluster stands – the aunts, uncles and cousins – then the rest of the boxes, then it spreads through the intermediate prices and up into the cheap seats under the trees. In a sweep of seconds, all 18,000 are on their feet, clapping away, and the Carpenters are smiling and bowing and that's the show.

The Reception. Where *are* they? Are they here? Midnight, everybody downing free cocktails at Bistro's bar – a nice rosy room with flowered-glass ceilings. Where *are* they?

Herb Alpert Tijuana Brass, at the center with a knot of seekers around him, looks at his watch, worried the kids aren't here.

The drinks are fine, but the smell of chiles rellenos and enchiladas wafting from the buffet draws a lot of the bar crowd in to dine. The rest wait drinking for the Arrival.

The publicist, who's racing around both rooms like Speedy Gonzales, gives you a quick aside on the way by: "Kids won't be able to talk to you much, big night tonight, pooped. Big success, too, notice? How many acts pull a standing ovation from 18 thou at the Bowl? Tell you what: Call the kids long distance, chat long distance with them next month when they come back from the tour. Good dealie-doo?"

You head for the enchiladas.

Most dining room people haven't heard of the Carpenters. They got an invitation from Stanley Kramer to hear about his new picture, and came over, is all. Is that who it's for, the Carpenters? Who are they?

In the middle of your second helping of food there's great tumult and shouting and popping of bulbs. The kids! Three couples knock over a table getting up, and streak from dining to the bar. The rest – including Stanley Kramer and his party and Arte Johnson and his – keep eating and telling stories.

In rushes the publicist, with red face, bulls across the dining room snorting. "Been looking for you. You should be out there. Get *near* them. The kids are really popping off, adlibbing about the concert and the career. Go on." He pushes your coat shoulder padding. "Go out there right now!" You tell him you can't; you've got to finish your chocolate mousse.

A half-hour later, as Karen enters through one dining room door you exit through the other. In the bar Richard is still holding forth for a following of five, describing how terrific, how outasight it went over tonight before the 18,000. The rest have backed off and are at side tables pouring down free Drambuies. When the inner circle diminishes to two, Richard bows out to dining, to a table of relatives, where Karen slumps in the head chair, frowning.

Arte Johnson and his wife leave. Stanley Kramer and his party leave. Herb Alpert Tijuana Brass leaves. Some gophers and back-up men stay boozing at the bar, pub-talking with agents, managers, PR men and wives. The lights lower, and next everybody's down Bistro's stairs and onto Canon Drive where it's a soft moonlit night in Beverly Hills.

Parked illegally in the lot next to Bistro crouches the Maserati. Almost dawn, the ritual begins anew. A residue of crowd collects around the kids' red car, all getting in the last word, the last shake, the last touch, before the kids finally break away, climb into the bucket seats and, with a mechanized roar, leave all the ordinary folks behind.

Can't We Stop?
Putting The Finishing Touches
On A Carpenters Record

By Dan Armstrong
Southeast News **(1971)**

How well performers do their thing under pressure is often the difference between success and failure. Karen and Richard Carpenter will have a new single on the radio Friday called "Hurting Each Other." They'll be finishing it tonight, Richard says. "Thursday morning," corrects Karen.

What the Downey pair will do tonight is put the finishing touches to the song, adding things none but the best-trained ears will even hear. But Richard hears, and Karen hears, and they are perfectionists.

Monday night they put in an evening session at A&M Studios, Herb Alpert's fantastically successful operation. To the average listener the song was already complete, and even those of us watching and listening were unable to perceive why the Carpenters would suddenly stop, say "no, that's not right," and start over again. It went something like this...

Karen: I want to make the "We ares" huge!

Richard: They are huge.

Karen: I want to make them huger.

Karen won. With a technician standing by, the Carpenters entered the sound booth and the 16-track tape containing their latest release was started. It will sound like 12 to 15 voices on the radio Friday, and all of them are Richard's and Karen's.

At the appropriate spot, the Carpenters each added a "we are" to the umpteen that were already there.

Richard: No!

Karen: What do you mean, 'no'?

Richard: Just what I said, no.

There was no anger, no exasperation. Richard had said it wasn't quite right and that was it. The tape started again, again they sang, again not quite right. Richard said "no." Finally he was satisfied, and they decided to work on a single word, "stop". The phone rang. Richard answered...

Richard: The organ's ready? What are we going to do with it? There's no room in here. Okay, bring it down and leave it in the hall.

Again, the Carpenters adjusted themselves behind a pair of microphones. The music started, and just as they started to sing, Richard suddenly stopped. "Hold it. Somebody's moving an organ out there." There were chuckles all around, and then back to work. "Stop" got the same treatment "we are" had before. After about three repetitions, none of them exactly right, Karen smiled. "It's a good omen," she said. "When it takes so long to get one right, watch out. Smash City."

When you hear "Hurting Each Other" Friday, it will last approximately three minutes. If you like easy listening, you'll probably like it. Richard Carpenter probably won't though. Undoubtedly he will find some little thing that "isn't quite right." That's very likely what put the Carpenters where they are.

Concert Review:
Riviera, Las Vegas,
September 22, 1972

Variety **(1972)**

When handsome brother-sis team of Richard and Karen Carpenter were warming up on the tune scene about 18 months ago, it was as opening act for Don Adams at the Sands; now that it's hot, it's top-lining at the Riv.

Carpenters' looks, sound, chatter and attitude are highly refreshing. Whether their primarily youthful fans will pause at the gaming tables remains to be seen.

Richard maneuvers in an ingratiating manner; he organs, duets with his younger sister (22) but wisely spotlights her role as lead singer. She's a charmer, has a fine, identifiable sound, and invariably wins over both youngsters and oldsters who are seeing her for the first time. One of their most ardent fans is in the latter category – their conductor Ray Bloch.

Carpenters do their trademarks, of course ("Close To You," "We've Only Just Begun") and offer such oldies as "Jambalaya" and such freshies as "Top Of The World" (their latest single). If trimming is in order, the medley of 1957-64 hit tunes could be chopped, perhaps in half, for good effect. They're backed by six of their own sidemen (Miss Carpenter's vocals are gracefully blended with her cocktail drumming) plus 19 members of the Jack Cathcart house orchestra.

The Choral Sound
Of The Carpenters

Frank Pooler
Choral Journal (1973)

It is well known that on their recordings Karen and Richard Carpenter sing all of the vocal parts using the overdubbing process, which was pioneered by Les Paul and Mary Ford in the late 1940s.

In a recording studio it is possible for two people to "stack up" as many vocal parts as desired, but at the present time Richard and Karen prefer to record in four-part harmony because that is what must be used on stage by the "in person" Carpenters group.

The comment, "you sound different or better on records," has never been heard from any of the millions of people who have seen and heard the group in concert. The usual audience and press commentary is that the "live" and the recorded Carpenters are identical in vocal sound. This parallelism is not an accident. Richard and Karen are determined that the "in person" vocal sound be of the same quality as that of their recordings. Previous to their first concert engagement in February 1969, Karen, Richard, Doug Strawn, Dan Woodhams and Gary Sims (the singing Carpenters) rehearsed seven days a week, twelve hours a day for six months.

Throughout this article reference is usually made to recordings because, while the "in person" Carpenters are not readily available, their recordings *are* and the vocal sound is the same.

The original Carpenters are highly skilled choral singers and were selected by Richard Carpenter for that reason. Their vocal ensemble sound is based on absolute vowel uniformity and a frontally focused brilliant "ē" vowel. The razor-sharp "ē" at the end of "Road Ode" ("roads of sorrow coming to an end for me") and the "we are" background to Karen's solo in "Hurting Each Other" are typical examples of the Carpenter tonal foundation. All of the other vowels and voiced consonants seek to maintain that knife-edged "ē" which is often produced while wearing what the group calls a "Disneyland smile." (Richard and Doug Strawn formerly performed at the Magic Kingdom.)

The "ah" sound used as a vocal background to instrumental solos in the fade-out choruses of "Goodbye To Love," "Help," and "Close To You," and the melismatic "oo's" in "A Song For You" and "Piano Picker," and the "wo's" in "Do You Know The Way To San Jose," possess the greatest possible similarity in vocal timbre to that "ē" which is produced when prefaced by an explosive "f" or "p" consonant. Those singers have both ear and breath control. Their rendition of "Love Is Surrender" gives but one example of the vocal control that can move an absolutely unified sound through all registers of the voice and from a soft to loud dynamic level with unyielding equality of color. The tonal unity commencing with the words "day after day as I wait for the man" from Richard's arrangement of Burt Bacharach's "Knowing When To Leave" is high voltage ensemble singing.

Carpenters also make frequent use of dramatic tonal change-up with an extremely breathy quality, which Richard calls "airy." It is produced by releasing a large amount of breath previous to the attack of tone. An audible exploding "h" in front of the word "I" renders a windy overcoating to the phrase "I may go wrong and lose my way" in "Do You Know The Way To San Jose." "Close To You," "Bless The Beasts And Children" and "Superstar" are a few examples of songs which utilize the soft, airy sound as vocal background in the slower moving ballads.

Carpenters move easily within this bright to breathy color spectrum. In "Baby It's You," the solo and ensemble quality changes from a pleading husky "many, many nights go by" to a harsh, biting "it doesn't matter what they say." These tonal contrasts are nearly always related to a change of textural mood and are dramatically convincing. They display that distinctive interpretive vocal coloring characteristic of the Carpenters style.

Richard speaks of two kinds of popular songs: those which can be delivered in a "conversational manner," where the vocal tone quality changes as contrasting moods are suggested in the lyric ("Baby It's You," "Superstar," "Bless The Beasts And Children"), and those songs with "neutral" texts and melodies ("Close To You," "For All We Know"), which do not demand dramatic emotional changes.

The December 23-30, 1972, issue of *Opera News* contained an article entitled "A Question Of Magic" by Denis Vaughan. Mr. Vaughan dealt with several techniques used by Sir Thomas Beecham in conducting Mozart operas. One of these techniques was to "add occasional accents, always organic and justified by the melody, but nearly always irregular and in asymmetrical patterns." Vaughan could have been writing about a particular stylistic tendency of the Carpenters. When they choose to use "irregular accents" they achieve them by exploiting the percussive power of certain consonants. The explosive power of the sharply accented "p's" in "pumpin'" and the savage hiss of the "s" in "gas" give to the phrase "and all the stars that never were are parkin' cars and pumpin' gas" (from "Do You Know The Way To San Jose") a sardonic, driving, pounding finish which contrasts sharply with the legato delivery of the lines which envelop it. Similar treatment is accorded the consonants "d", "ch" and "b" in "I'll Never Fall In Love Again" in the words "don't tell me what it's all about" and "out of those chains that bind you."

Unexpected accents frequently occur in the vanishing vowel of diphthongs ("walk on bah-ee"), and the second syllable of two-syllable words is often socked for dramatic purposes as in "never think-ing of my-self" from "Reason To Believe."

The Carpenters style often adds to this practice of irregular accentuation by inserting "w's" or "h's" before vowels within certain words and within melismas for purposes of accent (a device which had been used earlier by the Beatles and the Bee Gees). A few examples of this practice occur in "make it easy on yourself" (yourse-welf) and "don't tell me what it's all about" (abou-wout) from the "Bacharach-David Medley" and "think I'm going to be sad" (sa-had) from "Ticket To Ride."

The group also exploits the fact that some words "feel and sound good in the mouth" and they attempt to communicate that feeling and sound for its own sake as well as for making a word or phrase intelligible to their audiences.

An interesting use of "r" is discernable in Carpenters' performance. The harsh final "r" is, according to normal choral practice, omitted in "Mr. Guder" and the internal "r's" in "earth" and "birth" from "Crescent Noon" are de-emphasized to the point of omission. However in "Top Of The World" the "r" in "world" is given a purposeful country rasp and has caused several critics to wonder where Karen acquired a new accent.

Carpenters are concerned about impeccable intonation, blend, and balance. Their methods of achieving these choral basics are not unusual. Each member of the group possesses an unusually excellent sense of pitch and chordal balance. They strive for high thirds, exact octaves and perfect unisons. Thirds tend to be more prominent than fifths and very little vibrato is tolerated in the ensemble work.

63

All concerts are amplified. Unlike many pop groups who merely tap the microphone to see if it is "alive" and leave the balance to the sound engineer, Carpenters spend from a half to a full hour before each concert balancing first the voices and then the instruments and finally the combination. One member of the group is always out in the house and bears the responsibility for the sound balance. Richard attempts through his sound system to give each show, no matter what the acoustical condition of the hall, a large cathedral-like resonance.

Carpenter shares with other choral musicians the unending search for the right material. The easiest method for him, as for other choral directors, would be to wait and see what is a "hit" or what is working well for comparable groups. But he prides himself that his repertoire is distinctly his. Recently when another group recorded a song Carpenters were using in their show and the recording became a big hit, Richard withdrew the piece from his concert program rather than risk speculation that he was "cashing in" on someone else's success.

The Carpenter book has been culled from literally hundreds of songs and "demo" records sent to Richard from all over the world. When a song is finally selected for a Carpenter arrangement the first criteria must be that it gives him a strong emotional reaction; it has to raise "goose-pimples." The words of the song must also be appealing, not only to him but to what he conceives of the average record buyer. The lyrics can't be "far out" or suggestive because Richard feels strongly that the average buyer really doesn't care to purchase records with texts of this kind. The melody should be capable of sustaining varied harmonic support, and good possibility for choral arrangement must exist.

The Carpenters know what they like and why they like it. Their personal musical style has elicited a great deal of criticism from several rock critics who refer to their music as being "slick" and "superficial." But at concert after concert, the finest studio musicians in the business who come prepared for boredom lead the roaring standing ovations and leave praising the technical virtuosity and personal musical integrity of a group which has concertized throughout the world, has performed with the Minnesota Symphony, and has sold over twenty million recordings in a little over two-and-a-half years.

Richard and Karen are becoming interested in recording with larger vocal forces. A sixteen-voice children's choir was used on "Sing" and a sixty-voice choir will not only back Karen's solos but will be featured in contemporary compositions for choir alone in a forthcoming Christmas album.

Their influence is rapidly expanding. Music educators throughout the United States have been instrumental in securing Carpenter concerts for their localities and conventions. Both the American Choral Directors Association and the Music Educators National Conference have extended invitations to the group to share with them the choral sound of the Carpenters.

Frank Pooler is a professor emeritus at California State University Long Beach. He is respected in both academic and professional music circles as a leading authority on choral music. His association with the Carpenters dates from 1964 when Richard became accompanist for Pooler's CSULB University Choir. The two collaborated in the writing of "Merry Christmas, Darling" which has become a holiday standard. As Orchestral Director for the Carpenters, Pooler traveled with the group to Australia, Japan, Hong Kong and England, as well as Lake Tahoe, Reno and the White House.

Part Two:
Top Of
The World

It Happens In The
Middle Of The Road:
Confessions Of
A Carpenters Fan

By John Tobler (1974)

Not so long ago (a matter of months probably), there was a very distinct dividing line between music which appealed to rock fans and the more generally acceptable, bigger selling records bought by what is termed the "middle of the road" market. To a large extent, this barrier has now been broken down, in my view mostly because of two groups of performers, the now defunct Bread and the very much active Carpenters. In fact, the trend continues, a good example being the latest album by Andy Williams, where he is backed by the sort of musicians you might expect to find backing John Lennon.

Such a move is not the reason for the Carpenters' widening appeal, for even on their first album, *Ticket To Ride*, they had the help of Joe Osborn on bass, who has played on records for many of the west coast progressive groups over the years. It's my opinion that the duo's ability to appeal to most record buyers lies in the fact that they are able to select tuneful and catchy songs, and arrange and present them in a way that is not offensive to any but the most diehard avant-garde fan.

The start of my own appreciation of the Carpenters was hearing "Goodbye To Love," which was released as a single from their fourth album *A Song For You*. The tune must be familiar to practically everyone, and it's certainly one of Richard Carpenter's best compositions, but what made it so astonishing for me was the guitar solo towards the end of the record, which could easily have been played by some progressive hero of the ilk of Jimmy Page or Jeff Beck.

Many of my acquaintances were similarly impressed, and a number of people, myself included, could be seen stealing surreptitiously into our favorite record shops and whispering our requirements to an astonished assistant who probably thought we'd lost our minds. Shades of prohibition!

It was with great relief, then, that the news was received that the Carpenters next album would contain a long medley of pop hits of the sixties. To some this seemed to make Karen and Richard more acceptable, and while it may have alienated some of their older fans, who seemed to feel that such music was rather too noisy, it surely attracted a great many other people caught up in the curious phenomena of nostalgia, which seems to have gripped Britain during the last year.

If 1973 was the year in which you became anywhere between twenty-four to thirty years of age, there was a very good chance that you had the original singles which the Carpenters were recreating, or at the very least had heard them often enough for a chord to be struck in your memory.

It may be a sad comment on each of our lives, but the less complicated years of the early to mid-sixties certainly seem to strike a sympathetic chord in our minds, and memories of the Beach Boys in their original candy stripe shirts (black and white), and all those chanting girl groups like the Crystals and Chiffons seem to bring a smile to the most hard-nosed among us.

Now if the Carpenters had tried clever updating tricks with those songs of my heritage, I might not be writing this. But they didn't, and that medley on the second side of the *Now & Then* album is so affectionately performed that I'm really looking forward to seeing them perform live in England this February, when it's certain that they'll bring back a lot of happy memories to people like me.

Of course, not all that the Carpenters play comes into that revived category. Since acquiring the two albums I've mentioned, I've also become sufficiently interested to investigate their previous work, which for the most part is contained in three albums, chronologically *Ticket To Ride, Close To You* and *Carpenters*, and found that in each of them there is very definitely something which is quite specifically to my taste.

Perhaps to cater to latecoming Carpenters fans, a new album (*The Singles 1969-1973*) is being released to coincide with their British tour. As might be expected, this contains twelve of their biggest hits, which together make a very attractive proposition for the record buyer. I'm unable to detect a weak spot in the choice of material, although it should be noted that the aforementioned "oldies" medley isn't featured, as it is undoubtedly too long for inclusion, apart from the fact that it in no way fits the concept of the album.

However, the old adage about the only certain things in this world being birth, death and income tax can now be definitely rewritten – a fourth certainty has appeared, and that is that the Carpenters' new album and their European tour will be among the great successes of 1974. Actually, it's equally certain that I'll be there to watch.

Concert Review: Sahara, Tahoe, August 24, 1973

Variety (1973)

It's no secret that the Carpenters, with their tender songs of broken hearts and young love, have revolutionized the music scene and shattered trends to the far reaches of rock. They are wildly popular at the Sahara Tahoe and breathless approval is audible among under-30 customers.

Lyrics to some songs are pitched to adolescents and lush orchestrations occasionally pile up like whipping cream, but the sound is distinctive and sometimes touching, arrangements are sensitive, and Karen Carpenter handles her sure, melodious voice impressively.

Particularly in an era of flaming creatures and wildly mannered femme singers, Karen Carpenter, who sticks to the music, stands out. Her phrasing is controlled and stylized, harking back to band vocalists of the past. She holds her notes and sings the music as it's written, and the voice, while not of great range, is becoming a rich, well-seasoned instrument, pure and melodious within its limits.

Chief fault in her stage delivery is a distracting tendency to overact her songs. Voice is sufficiently expressive to allow her to stand motionless behind a mike, and it's unfortunate that nightclub pressures force her into unsuitable liveliness.

The Sahara Tahoe show, titled "Now & Then" after their latest album, is a satisfying blend of their best music and some pleasing forays into the tunes of the '50s and '60s.

"Rainy Days And Mondays," "For All We Know" and "Goodbye To Love" comprise bows to the past and loud applause greets their present hit "Yesterday Once More." There's also "Top Of The World" (recently made popular by Lynn Anderson), a country-style song, orchestrated in the group's style, and given Karen Carpenter's impeccable delivery.

Distinct separation of the show into old favorites and period medleys may seem anticlimactic to Carpenters fans whose biggest thrill is to see their big hits performed live. Oldies are solidly successful, with Pete Henderson participating amusingly as backup and with skill and assurance for solo and duet work with Karen Carpenter.

Tony Peluso, their lead guitarist, supplies amusingly overbearing D.J. intros, and Richard Carpenter, seldom heard as a soloist, acquits himself well with "Book Of Love." Otherwise, it's Karen Carpenter all the way, with fine versions of "Johnny Angel," "Leader Of The Pack," and "Runaway." Her "Jambalaya" is certainly different than more raunchy versions of the song, but the careful, stylized treatment is a pleasant alternative.

They have the good fortune to be supported by Skiles & Henderson, who add a lively note to this heavily musical show. Their comedy, with classic sound effects and unlikely props, plays well with their participation in the Carpenters' show, culminating with a wild, strobe-lit sword fight with drumsticks.

Soft Rock And
14 Gold Records

By Frank H. Lieberman

The Saturday Evening Post (1974)

Atypical hot Southern California afternoon. Smog. Bright sun. A bumper-to-bumper drive back from suburbia to the press agent's Beverly Hills office. ("You'll have no trouble writing about them. The few hours you just spent with them plus all that other time…")

Continual talk about how fantastic Richard and Karen Carpenter are added to the haze in the air. Every time a song finished on the radio, he pushed a button to find something else. "The commercials are awful." I was thinking more about food. My interview with the Carpenters, one of many the past few months, was at 11:30 a.m. It was now 3:00 p.m. They didn't feed me. I was starved.

Great. Honest. Real. Just normal kids. The adjectives continued to flow like a press release. So did the acid in my empty stomach. It was easier to nod in agreement. "If you need anything else, just call my secretary and she'll set up a phone call with them. I don't think you will, though; they did answer all your questions very completely and openly."

Finally. The Beverly Hills office. Downey – the Carpenters' retreat, about a thirty-minute drive from downtown Los Angeles – seemed a day's ride away. An ice cream store across the street. And no ticket on my car. It was worth it after all… I guess.

Listening to the tapes, I wondered what it would be like living in that fancy house with its luxurious Japanese garden and high, insurmountable wall around it. The wall wasn't really there… or was it?

"We've been called sticky sweet, Goody Two Shoes and squeaky clean," said Richard in an interview at the time of their first White House appearance. "But it's all relative, isn't it? We came along in '69 right in the middle of acid rock, when all the performers had this negative sort of 'take me as I am' attitude, never concerned about their stage appearance. And then we walk out, just normally clean. I mean, most people shower, right?"

Of course, that afternoon Richard and Karen had looked immaculate. They have every time I've been around them. Were they dull the first time I saw them at the Hollywood Bowl. It had to be one of the most boring concerts of all time. But that audience loved them. They cheered. And cheered. Two encores, if I remember correctly. My review wasn't very complimentary.

I looked up the telephone interview I had with them prior to that concert. Boy, did some of the answers illuminate today's session. Egads. Honest, real. All the press agent's (the same one all the four years) terms. I used them, too. Maybe, just maybe, he was right. Nah, nobody's perfect. Are they?

The career of Richard and Karen Carpenter is a story of blind faith, of being musical mavericks during the heyday of glitter rock, and of waiting and believing in themselves and their sound. (They sure do. I listened to other interviews with people ranging from an underground Los Angeles paper to a totally naive older woman's free-lance assignment. The answers were all the same, just like the way their music has been described.)

The Carpenters' music has been called by many labels – soft rock, easy listening, pabulum or homogenized rock. Critics shout it's commercial; others say it's reliable. But no matter. It's successful, and despite contrary claims, success is what it's all about.

Is that the key to the music industry? Dollars and cents? Do great sales dictate creativity? In many cases, yes. In the Carpenters' situation, I don't think so.

The Carpenters' popularity increased as reaction to harsh electronic hard rock began. In contrast to rock's loudness, the Carpenters' musical effect is to soothe, to pep up or to amuse. It is quieter using the same electric guitars, drums and horns as rock, but not as loudly. In contrast to the angry antiestablishment lyrics of so many rock songs, the Carpenters lean toward songs that talk about love in the rain or sitting atop the world.

At age twenty-seven and twenty-three respectively, the brother and sister combination claims fourteen gold records, three Grammy Awards and the loyalty of a huge contingency of fans.

Karen twirls her hair. Stares at the ceiling. Glances at the many gold records hanging on the wall. She was tired of the interviews the press agent had arranged. Sure, he was doing his job. But she was home. No airplanes. No Holiday Inns. She makes a face at the woman doing the interview, later saying, "I hope she didn't see me. But those questions! Who cares?"

Richard returns from escorting the woman to the door. Her time was up. I had another crack at them. But then, I was different (though the answers seemed the same). After all, I was writing a tribute (the Carpenters were paying for it) about Richard and Karen for a national record trade publication.

I kept picturing all the interviews and all the time I had spent with the Carpenters. It was late evening and I couldn't wait to finish transcribing the tapes.

Richard was explaining their success. "We've built a large following because it seems that the people understood us, and most critics didn't. [Me neither, at least at first.] I love rock. I enjoy Zappa, the Beatles and dozens more. [The shelves loaded with various types of albums proved his point.] I know we're not rock. We're pop. But we're not that kind of bland, unimaginative pop music that is so often associated with the term 'easy listening.' We don't just cover [copy] other people's recordings. I think we are a little more creative than that. We do our own arranging, our own orchestration. We try to bring our own interpretation to a song."

The perfect sound. Nah, nobody's perfect. Are they?

My wife reminds me of the late hour. "Just a few more minutes." Simple answer. Effective. Like the Carpenters' lyrics, I thought, but they are only words. Isn't there more to a performer, whether it be a solo artist or a group? Yes. Then couple the Carpenters' musical interpretation with their public relations image… and instant establishment success.

Soft rock stars, like the Carpenters, are proud to belong to the establishment. Right? Their lifestyle as well as their music reflects traditional middle-class American values. It's not personality that sells their records. I know for sure it's not their gimmicky theatrical antics on stage. They simply don't have any.

Maybe it's because Karen would rather eat a candy bar for quick energy instead of an amphetamine. Or maybe it's because they're made of sugar 'n' spice and everything nice.

Richard describes their image as "garbage. It has nothing to do with the music, how we record or play it. It's mostly garbage that came from the early literature. I never cared for it, and still don't… pushing this ridiculously clean image that hardly anybody fits."

Both claim they're "starting to overcome it." Judging by the editing of the record publication story they did, the process may be a slow one. Richard says that he and Karen "have reached the point where we can't hide our feelings just because somebody is not going to like it. We are expressing our minds and I don't think our thoughts vary much."

Life for Richard and Karen Carpenter is their music. It has given them everything they've wanted. They realize as entertainers they owe the public "something" for accepting their talents, but insist, "this doesn't give the public right to decide what we do with our lives or how we should think."

Richard cited an example, an incident in Tulsa that provoked his way of thinking. "We were rehearsing in a Tulsa auditorium and the air conditioning went out. Some people sneaked into the hall and noticed we had beer cans on stage. They wrote us a nasty letter saying how dare we drink beer, that they were appalled and that it changed their image of us."

Wouldn't those folks be shocked if they saw the inside of the lavish Carpenter home. There are a couple of well-stocked bars and a sensational wine collection. And there's even a pool table. Not the image of those pure, wholesome singers, that's for sure. If Karen hadn't answered the door once with her hair in curlers, wearing a long, blue robe with "SUPERSTAR" lettered across the back, I would have figured she slept in cellophane.

Richard and Karen are both concerned with their appearance, especially when it comes to publicity pictures. Watching them pick prints from a photo session is like a Looney Tunes cartoon. They can't be touching each other. "Someone might get the wrong idea. Like we were married instead of being brother and sister."

Richard is good-looking, according to a survey I conducted with some of my female friends. The males I checked with felt Karen was "a cute cookie who needed a new hairstyle and some different clothes." Karen's stage wardrobe is limited because of her first playing the drums and then coming to the front to sing.

But despite the limitations, the Carpenters' stage presentation draws capacity crowds throughout the world and usually excellent reviews. They magnificently recreate their record sound on stage. And again, Richard is the mastermind.

The Carpenters attempt to be perfect in their answers; so convincing. It leaves you wondering, is it all that good? There must be flaws. There's always gossip. But nothing is ever proven. Maybe it's different now since their folks moved to another house, built for them by Richard and Karen. Maybe now there are big, swinging parties.

I checked. There was… the usual gala Christmas party and then back on the road and more recording sessions.

Like thousands of other young Americans pounding away in basements across the country, the Carpenters turned on to the idea of making it big in the music business early. Richard started music lessons at age twelve and studied classical piano at Yale while the family was living in New Haven, Connecticut, where both were born.

While Karen's interest was in everything but music, Richard loved it all and had access to his father's extensive music collection, which included classics, big bands, jazz, Les Paul and Mary Ford, Red Nichols, and Spike Jones.

Richard's initial musical adventure was without Karen. He was sixteen "and only wanted a car."

"The first group I was in was horrible," smiles Richard, who also maintains a love for fast cars. "My hair was plastered back [he now, of course, subscribes to the dry look] and I wore glasses [now it's contacts only]," he explained. "With two guys in their twenties, we formed a group and got a job at a New Haven pizza dive… and were we horrible. I played the basic changes to most tunes and threw in arpeggios because of my technique. I was just learning substitution and just getting into improvisation."

The family's move to southern California ended Richard's fling, but it didn't take him very long to launch his West Coast activities.

It was 1963. Richard was a senior at Downey High School and continued his piano studies at the University of Southern California. He had hitched on to another group – similar to his previous one – and played at all the typical nightspots in the area.

Karen, the idol of thousands of girls for her cuteness, her career, and for having an older brother, started drumming when she was sixteen. Through subsequent group transformations, first as the Richard Carpenter Trio (with a friend), then as Spectrum, a larger band, she developed into the lead singer.

Spectrum had become "Carpenters" by 1968. Karen and Richard were doing all the singing, and they were still without a contract. Then in 1969, a friend of a friend of a friend, as Richard describes it, brought one of their tapes to Herb Alpert at A&M Records. He liked their work and signed them.

The Carpenters' first album was *Offering*, from which the single "Ticket To Ride" was released. The second LP was *Close To You*, which has sold four million copies.

Again it was Alpert who was the messenger from heaven, presenting them with the opportunity to record "Close To You."

Burt Bacharach had brought Alpert the song which he wanted the singer-trumpeter to record on his own. But Alpert decided against it because he didn't want to sing the line "sprinkled moon dust" and gave the lead sheet to the young Carpenters, who were rehearsing on an A&M soundstage.

Richard tells the story of how it sat on his piano for weeks before they recorded it. And some more incidents about their highly successful career, including their 1971 appearance on "This Is Your Life."

"I didn't even know who Ralph Edwards was," laughed Karen when recalling the television show. "And I didn't know it was back on the air," chimed in Richard. "We both thought it was a bit strange to be on that show," he added. "After all, we had only been in the limelight for six months at that time."

The Carpenters' success has sprung from Richard's devotion and belief in the unusual sound he created. He is the mastermind behind it all. Yet he isn't the star. In fact, on the early albums, despite doing all the work, he didn't receive any credit.

Does it bother him? "My end of the thing is not a whole ego-building thing as far as what the public realizes. Karen is the star. She's the one who gets the letters and requests for autographs. I don't get much attention, everyone's mostly interested in Karen... she's the lead singer and the featured part of the act.

"My end is selecting material, arranging, orchestrating, production, selecting personnel for the group, the order of the show and how to improve the show. They, the audience, don't realize what I do. They don't know I've written several hit songs; it's always Karen. Which is fine. But to me, I know what I've done. Even though a lot of people and critics don't like it, the fact is it's very commercial. It's well produced and it feels nice to me that I selected an unknown song and made it a hit. That makes me feel good, and sure, it feeds my ego."

The Carpenters' newest album is also Richard's product. It's entitled *The Singles 1969-1973* because he doesn't like the term "greatest hits."

"I feel it's really an overused thing," he says. "Individuals and groups with two or three hits all of a sudden put them on one album, use filler for the rest, and title it 'great.' This album contains eleven true hits, yes, but it wasn't just slapped together. We've remixed a few, recut one and joined a couple of others. It's simply something I feel we owe to our audience and ourselves.

"Music will always remain a part of our lives," says Richard. "How much of an impact we'll have is hard to say. Acts have gone up and set records, and then all of a sudden the public has had enough of their sound. They never totally leave, but they don't enjoy being at the top. It's not the happiest thing to think about, but it's fact.

"That's why I keep the public in mind and try to stay on top of all the successful products. I pay close attention to what our public seems to like and really respect their wishes. What so many critics and artists forget is that the public puts you on top and in the limelight. Going along with them isn't copping out, especially when you enjoy your music and what you're doing like we do."

Another thing Richard and Karen cited is that many people forget that they're normal people. "The rock thing has made so many people's thinking so freaky," says Richard. "We come along as average people and because we're not painting our face, and because we dress up for a performance, we're not hip. I know the music business is always searching for a new leader. Everyone 'who knows' claims there has to be something new and different. There has to be a new Beatles, or an attempt to make glitter rock the new trendsetter.

"Maybe there doesn't have to be something or someone new for a while. Sure, the '40s had Sinatra. In the '50s it was Elvis. The '60s belonged to the Beatles. So naturally something is expected for the '70s. And in trying to find that special thing, the oldies, the roots of rock, have been pushed into the limelight.

"I feel as long as everyone is searching, it just isn't going to happen. You can't manipulate success and tell the public, 'Look, here's your new leader.' When glitter rock hit, the 'who knows' were claiming it was the force of the '70s, While it's very successful it obviously isn't to the '70s what the Beatles were to the '60s. Obviously they were wrong.

"What these people don't realize is that Sinatra, Elvis and the Beatles still have the same magnitude today. They haven't faded... their makeup hasn't worn off."

The Carpenters:
An Interview

A&M Compendium (1975)

Editor's Note: Nearing the end of the sessions for their Horizon *album, Richard and Karen Carpenter were interviewed for a special issue of the "A&M Compendium," an A&M Records newsletter. What follows are excerpts from the conversation, which took place at Hollywood's Au Petit Café, in late March of 1975.*

I think a good place to start is with this album, which has been long time in the making. Where it is in relation to your earlier work?

Richard Carpenter: We're spending a lot more time, not just in selecting material, but in every last thing that has to do with the album. We're getting into a lot more stereo effects than the other albums had – things that have been happening lately in recordings, like stereo drums. We used to record the drums on two tracks – one track for the kick drum and another track for the rest of the set. We use four tracks now for drums, one for the kick, one for the snare, another one for the left tom-toms, and another one for the right tom-toms. In a lot of our recordings there has been a much thicker snare sound. We've really wanted to get into that and it takes time to EQ each different thing and experiment. Now we spend hours with the drums. We try them in a certain place, use a certain mike, listen to it, EQ it, get another mike, bring it in, try that out. Same with the piano. We played it in Studio D with the top almost down and a cover over it, then we rolled it into a booth that was meant for strings, to keep leakage down to a minimum, and opened up the top to see if the sound would be better, which it was. But all of this takes time.

Do you generally have a conception or is this a process of open-ended experimentation?

RC: Yes, it's that more than anything. I listen to a lot of records and I try to keep up with what's changing. I like to keep up with it – you don't *have* to, don't get me wrong. You can turn out an album that doesn't sound as good as *Band On The Run* or *Fulfillingness' First Finale*, and it's not going to make any difference whether it will sell or not, but it makes a difference to me.

Karen Carpenter: We've just spent a lot more time on everything.

RC: For example, I used a Harrison-style guitar part on "Yesterday Once More." Now if we use that effect, we'll record it once then go back and tune the guitar slightly flat, and then double the part – to give you a real nice spread, a fatter sound, and a sound that comes out of both right and left channels, but again, this takes time.

KC: We're into using different mikes for backgrounds, different mikes for leads. There's so much to get into, all the things that we never had time for, or stopped to take the time to get into.

It must piss you off sometimes, in terms of patience, having to wait for the right combination of elements before you can do the thing that you're really there for.

RC: That's one of the things I'm really there for, so *that* to me is as important as the actual performance. It doesn't frustrate me to do that. Also, we're recording at 30 inches-per-second which cuts down on your tape hiss, and we're going with Dolby right from the ground up, where we used to wait until we would go to the two track to use it – it makes for a very quiet recording. We're using 24-track too. Anytime you use Dolbys all the time, anytime you use 24-track all the time, being very sophisticated equipment, you have more breakdowns than you used to have. One breakdown at least per night, with one thing or another. The board, or the tape machine, the Dolbys, a mike or whatever.

And you just patiently go with it.

RC: The only thing that's frustrating is that you start worrying about the money you're spending after a while, and the time spent. If we had done this album like we did the other ones, it would have been finished, but we're going through a lot of changes and we're learning a lot of things, and I really find it to be a nice experience.

How close are you to finishing it?

RC: Oh, we're on a sustained forge. This last week we've picked up, so I would say we're about 85% done. We'll have it done by May 8th. We tried computer mix, we thought that would be a good idea, and it turned out not to be a good idea. Bet we blew two weeks on one song, "Solitaire." It just wouldn't go together, and we couldn't figure out why. I've never had that happen before. I've had times where I thought the arrangement was finished, and we'd go into mix, and then I would hear something else, and we'd run into a studio and put it on. But we're past that point. Everything was on it, and it still didn't sound right, and it turned out we just couldn't get the natural flow of the thing with the computer mix. You can just sit there and do one thing at a time. You may be getting two bars of piano that needs to be brought up at the end of the song, and you have to wait and let it go through the whole song, sit there and then raise it up and then start over.

KC: It was very boring. We never got the right feel.

RC: It took us two weeks to really find that out.

It's reassuring to know that human ears are still preferable.

RC: There's something spontaneous about doing it all at once. With 24 tracks, you need three people to mix it.

If you're really concerned with a quiet recording, I think what you really have to do is to supervise the mastering.

RC: Well, we have the top guy in town today – Bernie. I would never worry about it. I'll be there for the mastering, but he's great. The trouble is, after all the trouble and expense of going 30 Dolby and all this, the quality of the disc itself isn't so hot anymore. You get surface noise, even though you've gone through the trouble of making a totally quiet recording.

It's really maddening, because that's usually what you hear on a contemporary album. You don't hear the studio hiss in the tape.

RC: No, you hear surface noise. I bought an American *Band On The Run* with "Helen Wheels" and when I went to England, I got ahold of a British one and the difference in the quality is frightening. The English one is so much better. The American pressings are just terrible.

KC: They've gotten worse.

RC: Australia makes the best in the world, because they have such a little output, that they're hand checked. I went into the factory, and they have a woman that has a light and takes each album and checks it for flaws. Japan pressings are impeccable, and so are the English. I knew that for years. I had a friend who was going to England years ago, and asked me if there was anything that he could pick up for me, and I said please get me an English *Sgt. Pepper*, on Parlophone. I wanted to hear it next to the Capitol one, and even back then, before we got into the vinyl shortage and the quality trouble that there is now, the British pressings were much better.

It varies here from company to company.

RC: Yeah, A&M is better than normal; Elektra is very good, I'll tell you… MCA… I don't know if you've listened to any newer Elton John things, but the end of "Harmony" on the *Goodbye Yellow Brick Road* album, for example. I mean, the level of surface noise… I can't believe it.

So this will certainly be the most sophisticated Carpenters album.

RC: Yes, technically and performance-wise. Material-wise, I can't really say, unless I'm too close to it, that it will be all that much different. There's a lot of ballads, a lot of love songs, definitely, so that people that don't particularly care for our music, who consider it real sentimental or gooey, or whatever, are still going to feel that way, I think.

You're taking more time finding the tunes, right?

RC: Oh, yeah. Far more time.

What prompted you to do that?

RC: I just got into this thing where I wanted every song to be strong enough to be a single. We've already got two on *Horizon*. "Solitaire" is a single, "Desperado" is a single, "Goodbye And I Love You" is a single, and I think "Happy," which we didn't think was until it was finished, is strong enough to be a single. What I'm getting at is that there are six or seven songs that could be singles. They aren't going to be, but that makes for a damn good album.

Is that your prime criterion in selecting the tunes?

RC: I like things that don't sound like fillers, throwaway cuts or whatever. I like to find songs that I can do a decent arrangement on, that I can feel inspired by when I hear the tune, and tunes that the people who buy your records are going to like. The Bacharach-Davids aren't together, the Williams-Nichols aren't together. People we used to get some material from, they're not writing together anymore, so it makes selecting harder.

KC: There was a period when we were looking and there just wasn't anything we wanted to cut.

RC: Then all of a sudden, two or three things came along.

KC: So that's why it took so long.

RC: I've selected a lot of songs that really go down into Karen's lower register, because I think she really sounds good that way.

The first note on "Only Yesterday" is low. I was real impressed with the single, because it is so free of any sort of gimmick; it's just a real straightforward song.

RC: I was trying to write a song that had the feel of the sixties. The castanets, the chimes, and yet part of it has a sound of the seventies, the spread of the guitars, the saxophone through tape delay.

Who's the sax player?

RC: Bob Messenger. He's played on all our records. He's in our backup group. The guitar is Tony Peluso.

Richard, I recall that you had a really interesting definition of soul, in reference to some criticisms about your music, and other people's music, for that matter.

RC: To me, soul is a word that can be applied to all forms of music. Soul is feeling. And soul doesn't have to necessarily mean black feeling. So a critic may not like our music and says it has no soul. It sure as hell does have soul in its own way. It doesn't have, maybe inflected black soul, like Gladys Knight or whatever, that type of thing that soul has come to mean. What I'm getting at is Joan Sutherland has soul when she sings opera. Tchaichovsky had soul... he most definitely did when he composed. So did Rachmaninoff or Fats Waller, or it can go on into a hell of a lot of different directions. And our music, in its own way, has as much soul as Gladys Knight or Stevie Wonder. It's just not the same type. What you're referring to is that article that said that Olivia Newton-John is so lacking in vocal definition that she actually made us sound like we had soul. It's a ludicrous statement. Soul isn't just something black. To me, Cole Porter, Irving Berlin, Burt Bacharach, Paul Simon have plenty of soul.

The word has just been overused and misused, which is something the critics have missed in your music, extending the meaning of soul.

RC: I think so. A lot of our music is judged by rock standards. It shouldn't be compared to rock. It's pop. It's not pop like Muzak pop. See now that's another thing. If you're going to put us down, that's okay. People are entitled to their opinions. One of the English pieces said, and it's a tired cliché by now anyway, that we sounded like Muzak. That's really tired stuff, to call somebody you don't like who's easy listening "Muzak." I think somebody mentioned about David Gates' first album, that it's the same old Muzak stuff. That's not true. Muzak, if they're going to get into saying that, doesn't even have any vocals. It's all instrumental. We have some fairly strong backbeats and a lot of things that would definitely not get played over that at all. Maybe next to Grand Funk, or Led Zeppelin, or whomever, it seems very quiet, but next to Muzak, it sure as hell isn't quiet.

KC: It's the same as us being termed "easy listening."

RC: It may be true, but it's progressive in it's own pop way. In other words, we introduce songs. Easy listening artists will cover whatever's been done. You'll get three or four easy listening albums a year that are nothing but covers of what's been in the Top Ten the past two or three months. They're thrown together. Some arranger does them. A producer picks the stuff, they get an arranger, the vocalist comes in and puts the whole album together in two or three days, and they throw it out and call it *Tie A Yellow Ribbon* or *Rainy Days And Mondays* and *Sing*. Songs that John and I wrote – like "Yesterday Once More," "Goodbye To Love," "Top Of The World" – got a lot of covers. It's not your average easy listening act by any means.

I don't think your music has been characterized that way because of a lack of artistry but because of its accessibility. The kind of music you are alluding to is accessible to people because of a familiarity with the tunes. And your music, even though it's fresh material, has an immediate engaging quality. You're working with conventional forms.

RC: Oh sure. It's standard-type stuff. I never said it was all that different.

There's something to be said for working within the limitations of convention or a particular form.

RC: It has a sound. You know it's us as soon as you hear it.

I think the fact that your records are so successful established them as an institution better and faster than any other artist in the world. When you put a record out, within three months, it's an established part of our culture.

RC: Most become standards. Granted, "Postman" isn't going to be, and maybe this new one won't be either. Take a look at "Close To You," "We've

Only Just Begun," "For All We Know," "Rainy Days And Mondays," "Hurting Each Other," "Sing," "Yesterday Once More," "Top Of The World," "Won't Last A Day," they've become standards. The least successful went to number 12. "Ticket To Ride" didn't do well, but since "Close To You," there hasn't been one that's gone below 12. And ten of them so far have been million sellers. And ten of them have gone Top 3. "Superstar" didn't get too many covers, because of the lyric content, I guess. I know Vicki Carr did it. But there weren't that many vocalists that did "Superstar."

Did you ever really get annoyed or fed up with the whole critical thing, the misconception of you, and said 'Well, if that's what they want, I'll do a rock and roll album'?

RC: Hell, no. I don't take critics seriously. We couldn't do a rock and roll album that would sound right. That's not our thing. I love rock. It's not like you can turn around and say, okay let's do a rock and roll album, because there's no way we could do it justice. It wouldn't sound right.

Your music has undergone a dramatic reevaluation by the rock press. When the Singles *album came out people were calling us up and asking for a copy of the album. They were embarrassed at first because they liked rock and roll, they liked things that they could talk about in print without going out on a limb. And then the reviews of that album, when they came in, were much more positive. I think what happened was all those songs were a part of everyone's lives because they were on the radio in the cars. Together they made a very deep impression on people. And they said, "Oh, yeah, some of that stuff is really good." The Singles* album revealed a technical efficiency of arranging and writing, and with a series of singles. But when it was all there on a record, that brought together a lot of different elements, the reviewers began to understand. You made a comment, Richard, about putting all the singles on one album, which hadn't really been done up until that time.*

RC: Yeah. First of all, if you're lucky enough to be able to split it up and actually have an album with everything on it a hit, which very few people have, it would be divided into two volumes. Bread, two volumes. Creedence Clearwater, where they could have had an album beautifully done with all hits, had two albums. We were the first to put them all on one.

Did you remix any of the songs?

RC: Oh yeah. We recut "Ticket To Ride" from the ground up, remixed "Hurting Each Other," most of them.

Do you think the critics understand the complexities of what it takes to put out a Carpenters song?

RC: No. Because they always say our music is not complex. I still don't know what they're getting at. They should be there when we're putting it together. It's anything but simple.

There is a hell of a lot going on in something like "Only Yesterday." Arrangement wise, different colorings, it would get technical and boring to explain how many different things are on that record. And how much time is put into it. Not only the engineering, but in the arranging as well.

Have you ever wanted to produce someone else?

RC: No, I don't have the time, so I don't give too much thought to it.

What are your own musical tastes in records, either sonically or in terms of the aesthetic in pop music and rock and roll.

RC: My favorite group is the Beatles. American group – Beach Boys. Mothers of Invention, I've always liked. Steely Dan and a lot of others. I know I'll leave out someone. Doors. David Gates. I think some of his things are incredible. His voice is incredible. Not really heavy music, but damn nice pop music. Elton John, although I like his earlier stuff better. Neil Diamond. Always a Nilsson fan. Randy Newman.

Do you like the Byrds?

RC: Oh, I think they were terrific.

What singers do you like, Karen?

KC: As vocalists, I think Streisand is unbelievable. Dusty Springfield. Ella Fitzgerald.

RC: You see, I'm leaving people out like Oscar Peterson, Spike Jones. Red Nichols.

KC: Bing Crosby, Perry Como. Dionne Warwick.

So you have a well-stocked record cabinet.

KC: Very wide selection. Almost forgot earlier Presley. My taste naturally evolved from what Richard liked. I was totally into whatever he listened

to. But my dad was into classics and pop, not rock. He was more into vocalists, like Crosby, Como, crooner types.

When did you first start writing?

RC: I started when I was in the eighth grade. Started writing with John [Bettis] in 1967. A lot of things that were on the first couple of albums were written by us back into the sixties.

Do you feel like you're into a highly creative period of time now as a writer?

RC: Absolutely not. It's nice that everything we've written from "Goodbye To Love" on has become a single, and a hit. But there haven't been that many new songs. But back in the late sixties, we didn't have albums to record or roads to go on. We had this gig at Disneyland, and we used to spend time there writing songs. We got fired from our gig at Disneyland. We weren't very company-oriented. The songs are now more commercial than they used to be, but they aren't being turned out in numbers like they used to. Between production, touring, and all the business, I find it really hard to write.

What are your reviews like of your concerts?

RC: Fifty-fifty. They very rarely even get into the music at all. The reviews concern themselves with audience dress, the fact that there aren't that many blacks there, etc. They complain about the way the stage looks, which is ridiculous. One person showed up at the sound check in the afternoon, and did a review of the sound system.

Do you like performing?

RC: Oh, yeah.

KC: We know what's right and what's wrong with our performance. There are some nights that no matter how hard you try, it just doesn't go right. Ninety percent of the critics you run into, they walk in and they have already judged you before they've even seen you. They might as well print the article before coming.

Has it changed any in the last few years?

RC: No. Only the *Rolling Stone* piece. Finally, someone presented a nice – not all pro, but not snide – objective article. I couldn't believe it when I read it. I really felt that it was good.

How do you feel about being one of the top five guaranteed acts in the country?

RC: I'm proud of it. We work hard at our career. I think it's something to last five years. The new album and single are doing really well. All the concert business is doing fine. Things in Japan are even better than when we went over there. It's bigger in England than before.

You probably rank higher getting a record on the Top 40 than anyone.

RC: I think it's Elton John and us. I'm really proud of that.

KC: It's an unbelievable feeling to have things like that happen. We never look at it as a sure-fire thing. We never take it for granted that anything will make it.

RC: I read an article on Elton John where he's really on his singles and what is happening with them. I sure as hell do worry about that too. He calls radio stations and checks chart listings. And that's the way we stay on top of it. I love the business end of it. I really like singles. I think the single is really an important thing, even though it doesn't make you the kind of money an album does.

The magical thing about singles is that they are so concise – you have two or three minutes to say something different – to have an impact on people. It's one of the most concise mediums of expression.

RC: There are not that many artists that have had one hit single after another. When the price of singles went up, the sales went down. Singles are made out of such crappy material that it's unbelievable. Distortion, everything. It's trash compared to albums. If you want to make money off a record, you should make it off an album. Not a single. Save them for promotional things. Never think about royalties and money coming from a single. Even though we sell quite a few. To me, it's to help the album. The *Song For You* album did two million and *Close To You* did more like four. If "Top Of The World" had come out instead of "It's Going To Take Some Time", the *Song For You* album would have done another million units. It was a stronger single than "Goodbye To Love" was. *Close To You* had two monster hits on it to promote it. And the tan album was one of two that had three gold singles off of one album. Blood, Sweat and Tears' second album, with "Spinning Wheel," "You Made Me So Very Happy," and "And When I Die" was the other one. *A Song For You* had "Hurting Each Other" but "Hurting Each Other" came out four months before the *Song For You* album came out, so it was already an oldie. "It's Going To Take Some Time" went to 12, which is nice, but not compared to what our other records did. "Goodbye To Love" went to seven, which again was nice, but wasn't a million seller. It took up to "Top Of The World" to get a smash record off of that album. And it upsets me because that's my favorite album of ours. I wish it had done better. If "Top" had just come out at the release time of *A Song for You,* it really would have sent that album higher than it went.

Don't you think it's all a point of timing, in getting the single out at the right time?

RC: Absolutely. The single got Elton John back. The *Elton John* album and *Tumbleweed Connection* did very well but *Madman Across The Water* didn't do as well. Same with Neil Diamond and the *Stones* album. It had "I Am, I Said" in it, but again, like "Hurting Each Other," "I Am, I Said" was released months before the album, so it was an oldie by the time *Stones* was released. Neil Diamond was like us. He would sell a certain amount of albums but if he had a hit single, he would sell more albums. Then he came out with "Song Sung Blue" and that did it. That came out and then the album *Moods* went number one. The Elton John live album didn't do well. The *Friends* album didn't do well. And he had several singles, like "Levon" and "Friends" and "Tiny Dancer" and "Border Song" and ones that weren't doing well at all. I mean they were long and they weren't getting too much airplay and they didn't go Top 30. I liked *Madman Across The Water.* I really thought it was terrific. But it didn't do all that well, compared to some of his other things, because he hadn't had a Top 10 record or a Top 20 record since "Your Song". He went a hell of a long time without a hit single and then "Rocket Man" came along. "Rocket Man" went to seven, which is only as high as "Your Song" went. Compared to his new records, that's really nothing. Like "Lucy" or "Don't Let The Sun" or "Philadelphia Freedom."

"Crocodile Rock" was the one that got him the crossover play.

RC: But album-wise, *Honky Chateau* went sailing right up to one because of "Rocket Man." Look at Roberta Flack... "Killing Me Softly." She had this huge, big hit with it, but she waited months before she got the album out, and it went to three. I'm not saying that's bad, but I'm saying if it came out as "Killing Me Softly," the single, was peaking, it would've done better. Now she's putting out a *Feel Like Making Love* album, when the single, "Feel Like Making Love," was a hit six months ago.

You might say that you guys do the same thing.

RC: Sometimes. I wish we had had the *Song For You* album when "Hurting Each Other" was one, but we didn't. "Postman" was number one in three trades at the same time. The ideal thing would have been to put out the *Horizon* album the week that "Postman" went to one.

So your greatest success has been in developing the single both as an art form and as a commercial entity.

RC: Yeah. How many people can you name – and I'm not on an ego trip, this is a fact – that have had hit singles one right after another after another? It's a type of thing where it takes a certain talent to be able to pick something that becomes a hit single. You used to hear "Well, you've gotten to that point that no matter what you put out…" Bullshit. Harry Chapin followed up a number one smash with a number 43 without-a-bullet record. Neil Diamond would do it consistently. A Top 10 (hit) and then he'd put out "Soolaimon" and it would go to 30. Then he'd put out something that would go Top 3, then he would put out "He Ain't Heavy, He's My Brother," which would go to 20. Then he would put out something that would go Top 5, then he would put out something that would go to 14. Each record has to stand on its own. The Beatles did it. Creedence did it until they split. The Jackson Five did it for a while. But we've been going now for five years, with 14 consecutive Top 12 records, and I really am proud of that.

Your first album, Ticket To Ride, *is interesting. It sounds like a lot of sixties groups. Not exactly psychedelic, but sort of ambitious.*

RC: That album, I had, in my mind, finished years before we got the contract. That wasn't where I was at the time we signed, and some of it could have been a lot better, but you can hear that the ideas were there. Time signature changes, extended solos, and things that we don't do now. I should've just forgotten it and gotten down to where I was at the moment. But it was like I had to do that album. I didn't care if we had gotten signed in 1980. That was what the first album was going to sound like. And that's what we did. And that's why there is such a big difference between the *Ticket To Ride* album and the *Close To You* album. I just happened to hear something from it the other night on KNX and got out the album and listened to it, and it's really different than the other stuff we've done since.

People still say around the country that if you redid "Ticket To Ride," it would be a number one record.

RC: Yeah. We redid it for the *Singles* album and it's right where it should be, but I don't know about releasing anything more that's old, after "Won't Last A Day."

Are you going to put out "Desperado"?

RC: I don't know yet. It doesn't matter, but I don't think the rock people are going to dig it at all. Our stuff is polished, because I believe in production, and all. They'll probably call it slick.

That track has an emotion and intensity that is new to your style.

RC: I think so, too. I hope you're right.

KC: The same thing happened with "Desperado" that happened with "Superstar". That song had been around and been done by a few people.

And lyrically, as far as that goes, people don't remember that "Superstar" is about what it's about.

RC: Well, we had to change that one line, or it wouldn't have been a hit. "Hardly wait to sleep with you again," which I think she put in just for shock value. I changed it to "be" with you. It never would have gotten to the Top 40 otherwise. Now you can get away with "made love in my Chevy van," and Simon can get away with "making love with Cecelia in my bedroom," but he couldn't get away with "crap in high school." They made Lou Christie recut "Rhapsody In The Rain" because he said "making love in the rain." And "in this car love went much too far" had to be changed to "love came like a falling star." It still got the point across.

Remember he used to have a fortuneteller to tell him what singles to release? And he wrote some single about her.

RC: "The Gypsy Cried". That was right before "Two Faces Have I."

They have testing services now.

KC: What is that?

RC: For "goose bump reaction"?

Have they ever tested a Carpenters record?

RC: I don't know. See, now they have "goose bump effect." That's the thing that Robert Hilburn is missing. He's into lyrics. He's not into music. I doubt he could ever get a chill from music. Look what he has to talk about. I really like lyrics. Newman's lyrics, Joni Mitchell's and many more. But hell, it's a chill factor that comes with good music. You can get off on a song for its feel or its raunchiness – like I really got off on "Black Dog" and "Whole Lotta Love." You don't get a chill from that, but you get something else. It's really hard to describe. Like "Bridge Over Troubled Water" – you get a chill. At least I do. But I think that judging from the rock critic's point of view, they never get that... the sheer beauty of the music.

It's not just the words, "Sail on silver girl," but it's everything that's happening in the song at that moment.

RC: I'm glad you brought that line up. It chills – beautiful.

KC: The bridge in "Old Friends."

RC: Chills in "Something So Right". Maybe you wouldn't get from "Kodachrome" but you still dig it for different reasons. You brought up two lines that got to you, both lyrically and musically. "Desperado" is a chill song, both the music and the lyrics. It's there. It's there in a lot of these rock acts, even though they concentrate on other things. The Eagles, even though they're not a hard-rock act, wrote a song like "Desperado." It's like a spiritual. Something that was written 200 years ago. I just think there are people that are just not touched musically and that's what I'm getting at with soul. There's soul in the music we've brought up. Not black soul, but it's soul. It's right there.

Horizon

By Tom Nolan
A&M Compendium (1975)

The Carpenters have finished recording what is in many ways their most ambitious album to date: *Horizon.* The technology alone has consumed a great deal of energy, with scores of separate mikings making the production definitively "state-of-the-art."

But above, before, and beyond the sound – which Carpenters' aficionados will expect to be impeccable anyway – is the music. Some of it is already familiar to us: the hit singles "Please Mr. Postman" and "Only Yesterday." (Notice how easily and quickly the Carpenters made the transition from the unblinking optimism of "We've Only Just Begun" to the sweet wistfulness of "Yesterday Once More" and "Only Yesterday"; apparently the existential distance was never that great.)

Other tracks include a 1949 Andrews Sisters tune, "I Can Dream, Can't I," which features the Billy May Orchestra, a song Richard's collaborator, John Bettis, considers their best-ever composition, "(I'm Caught Between) Goodbye And I Love You," a four-and-a-half-minute version of Neil Sedaka's "Solitaire," and – most exciting of all – the Don Henley/ Glenn Frey ballad, "Desperado." Richard is expecting the biggest critical sneers yet when the latter track is released, because of its "underground" popularity (though a highly respected song, it has not yet been a hit single). He may be happily surprised. A critical reevaluation of sorts seems to have begun with the release in late '73 of *The Singles*, the Carpenters' greatest hits collection.

Whether or not "Desperado" gains the nod from *Rolling Stone*, it certainly will please those attuned enough to Karen and Richard's work to be appreciative of exciting developments in it. Karen's singing on this track is especially moving; she utilizes a hitherto-unheard lower register, with startling effectiveness.

Horizon is about to be released as I write this. I have a hunch it's going to make my summer.

Concert Review: Riviera, Las Vegas, August 24, 1975

Variety (1975)

Karen and Richard Carpenter, with backup quintet, have firmed up their previous mushrock displays into a more solid overall presentation. Current fortnight with Neil Sedaka is the best combination for them so far and in musical selection the Carpenters' roster is put together very well. Audience reaction is overwhelming at times.

Karen Carpenter, fortunately, is out front from her onetime scrunched position behind drums, moving around, communicating well in song projections and friendly girl-next-door talk. But, she is terribly thin, almost a wraith, and should be gowned more becomingly. Brother Richard is a confident leader from his keyboards, directing Cubby O'Brien on drums, Dan Woodhams on bass, Tony Peluso on guitar and organ, Doug Strawn on amped clarinet and Bob Messenger, reeds. Dick Palombi takes his cues to direct the strings and other sections of his orchestra. Put together, the sound is full when needed, lean as required, with the total orchestral finale a most effective affirmation at curtain.

Sedaka generates enough excitement in his opening 40 minutes to indicate future headline status. His in-person ambience is so very much different from the almost effete manner with which he purrs on discs. The live Sedaka's warbling quality is potent, and filled with nuances. He moves well, can shout and boogie along with the best of them, and in the Carpenters' seg, when he reappears with Karen to belt out "Superstar Medley" of the '50s and '60s, the session really fires up. During his opening period, seated at the keyboard, he puts out hit after hit and gets his crowd up and yelling on "That's When The Music Takes Me," prompting a standing ovation.

Middle America Personified?
Carpenters Fight The Image!

By Ray Coleman
Melody Maker **(1975)**

Richard and Karen Carpenter have decided to fight their whiter-than-white image and declare themselves as "ordinary folk who take a shower and yet get bad-tempered like anyone else." In a six-year build-up to their current status, the Carpenters have achieved plenty but said little. Their music is straight pop, with little rock connections. "Do we have to apologize for that?" demands Richard.

Karen Carpenter is a student of needlepoint and makes cushions. She finds it relaxing, especially on the road during those interminable journeys. Richard Carpenter is an enthusiast of fine wines, and knows a good year. He's been known to choose a restaurant only because of its wine list. He even smells the corks. Neither of these two characteristics will help the Carpenters' reputation in the area they seek to conquer: the gentle persuasion of the self-appointed hip.

But then, it's hardly what they do or even look like that's caused Richard and Karen to sell nearly 30 million records, including ten gold singles and five gold albums. It must be something to do with their music. And breathes there a man with soul so dead that he cannot accept their recorded beauty?

When the book on popular music of the 1970s comes to be written, the Carpenters should figure mightily in the chapter on quality music. It's been said that the blandness and safeness of their sound is in line with the uncertain times in which we live, and with the post-Nixon determination of President Ford for everything to be super-wholesome and non-controversial. Middle America personified. That's perhaps partly true, but the shame here is that Carpenters music seeks no categorization and waves no flag for anything except excellence.

Their music transcends barriers. And yet, while rock itself has been allowed to settle into music making with little outward message – the voices of revolution have long subsided, or at best have a hollow ring – the straight contemporary pop of the Carpenters is not allowed by many rockers to exist without a great deal of sneering.

Fine music alone isn't enough apparently. Richard Carpenter's short hair and his sister Karen's girl-next-door appearance don't equal rebellion or, indeed, take any stance at all except that of creative, melodic pop musicians. Thus, we have the increasingly wide gulf between public taste and the hard-line radicals who want change – an end to conservatism. And still the Carpenters claim audiences right across the age spectrum: their recently canceled British tour was to emphasize that their audiences stretch from age nine to 90, and that classy music in any form will never go out of style.

Excellence in all forms of music demands recognition, and it seems to me that the Carpenters – quite aside from their restatements of fundamental values in popular music – represent standards which should never become blemished by irrelevant commentaries on their appearances. Many artists of sheer genius, after all, have hardly looked hip.

Meeting the Carpenters, one becomes acutely aware that they are hurt by the knocks which have unnecessarily overshadowed their success. Yet nobody produces all those gold records without intense dedication. Undoubtedly the nervous energy expended by Karen was responsible for her collapse and cancellation of the British tour. For six years, she had been playing the role of "just another member of the band, the one who sang." Feminists may choke and chauvinists will laugh, but the reality proved otherwise, according to her boyfriend Terry Ellis (he's also their manager now, and regular *Melody Maker* readers will remember that he's the manager who steered Jethro Tull). "Girls just can't take that life without something going wrong." Ellis observed.

From "Close To You" and "We've Only Just Begun" through to "Please Mr. Postman" and "Desperado," the Carpenters have given us peerless popular music. And remember, even though they work in the pop area, most of their work is self-composed and arranged by Richard with spectacular precision and inventiveness.

It's worth remembering, in this latter half of the seventies, that for the opportunist who fancies a hit and is blessed with a good ear plus some vocal/instrumental talent, there's a gigantic catalogue of many thousands of good songs that can be converted into hits. No need to go to much trouble writing and arranging. Flip through the archives and recycle an oldie! The Carpenters have not relied on this safe method, but have produced quality popular music.

KAREN: I WAS ALWAYS A LONER
On Playing Drums

What's more important to you, singing or playing drums?

Karen Carpenter: They're both special to me. I love to play, I really do. When I started there were very few female drummers, but I didn't start playing just to be a gimmick. It was different and I realized it was something new, but at the same time I took a lot of pride in knowing how to play my instrument.

People will ask me, "Is it hard to play and sing at the same time?" No, because it was something that just came naturally. For the first year and a half to two years we were on the road, I played the whole show and I never thought twice about it. I didn't need anyone to do my playing, just like I didn't need anybody to do my singing. But as we got bigger and Richard started to realize that there had to be somebody fronting the group, I happened to be the only girl in the group who was doing the lead singing. Everybody was looking at me. And I said to Richard, "Oh no you don't," because it hurt me that I had to get up and be up front. I didn't want to give up my playing. So singing was an accident. Singing seriously came long after the drums.

I definitely take drums seriously. I have five sets of drums. When we finally made the decision to get another drummer we were very picky about who we got. I like a certain style of playing and I wanted somebody who played like me, because that's what we were used to. And we've always been lucky with drummers.

Do you practice the drums? Do you study other drummers?

KC: I haven't practiced since the day we went on the road. No time. When I first got my set I was 16. I played for a year before I ever studied. I just picked it up. It was something that just absolutely came naturally. It just felt so comfortable.

But I will not play drums quite so much on stage in the future. When we went on this past summer tour, Richard decided he wanted me up front the whole time, just to get a different look.

I do want to play, but we're going to treat my playing as something special, rather than just having me ending up as the drummer that's backing up the group. There's a way to do it properly and that's what we're going to do, because I do want to play. Absolutely. (At this point Carpenters manager and Karen's boyfriend Terry Ellis interjected: "Over my dead body.")

On Her Voice

At what point did you actually sing your first note and why? How long was the drumming without singing going on before you sang?

KC: When I was about 13. I can't really remember why I started to sing. I really don't. It just kinda happened. But I never really discovered the voice that you know now, the low one, until later, when I was 16. I used to sing in this upper voice and I didn't like it. I was uncomfortable, so I think I would tend to shy away from it because I didn't think I was that good and I wasn't. But I hear tapes now of my lower voice and you can tell it's me but I sound country!

It's kinda corny to listen back. We had an original recording of Richard's songs that I sung and the range was too big. I'd be going from the low voice to the high voice and even though it was all in tune, the top part was feeble and it was different – you wouldn't know it was me.

Then suddenly, one day, out popped this voice and it was natural. When I was in college, the chorus conductor was a very big influence on Richard's ideas of putting a vocal group together. He heard this voice and he wouldn't touch it. He said I should not train it. It doesn't need training. It's arty and natural. And the only thing I did work with him on was developing my upper register so I would have full, three-octave range. So it really helps.

You'll only hear me "up" on records as a background. Like in "I'll Never Fall In Love Again" there was a 13-part chord that covered three octaves and it took Richard's lowest note and my top note to get it. Richard also has a great falsetto, so between the two of us we can practically cover anything. Something else you don't think about is being able to sing in tune – thank God I was born with it! It's something I never thought about. When I sing, I don't think about putting a pitch in a certain place, I just sing it.

What singers are you particularly in awe of?

KC: I always liked Ella Fitzgerald, Nilsson, and David Gates has one of the best male voices ever. Perry Como is absolutely fantastic. I like Dusty Springfield, Dionne Warwick. A lot of different types of singers, and for different reasons.

Do you want to be remembered as a classic singer? A lot of people regard your voice as one of the best in popular music. Do you really regard yourself as someone to be remembered in the history of popular music?

KC: I sure hope so. I'd be a fool to say no. That is the ultimate compliment, to have respect not only from your fans but also your peers and other singers. To have that kind of a reputation and to have it to stay, it would be fantastic and it's really nice to know that other people think that something you yourself have is that special. It's a great feeling.

The Business

KC: You have to watch everything you put out and with each hit you get you have to work five million times harder. Anybody who believes that line about "I have my hit record, now I'll just put out the same track with a different lyric over it," they go up and down so fast you can't even remember their names. It's their own dumb fault because anybody who treats the business that way doesn't deserve to be in it.

This isn't a game, you know, it's a highly respected, smart business. NOBODY knows until a record goes out, it's played and they buy it. Very few are just automatic, out-and-out smashes and if you get one in your entire career you're damned lucky. Once you've got the one you pray for the next one. And every time a record comes out we watch every radio station that picks up on it – day by day, reports, charting, numbers, sales – because that's our business. There's not a day that goes by that we're not buried in the charts of the music papers. The competition is unbelievable. We keep watching what we're up against.

There's not that many that have come through and are just banging in there every time they come out with a record. The Beatles, the sheer pleasure of the Beach Boys coming back, they're excellent. Utter heaven. I mean, just knowing there's a Brian Wilson around is enough to make you go to sleep at night. I mean it. Genius is walking around.

One who's very upsetting is David Gates. He's so overlooked, so incredibly talented. He not only writes his tail off, but that voice, my God, it's gotta be one of the all time greatest male voices ever. After he left Bread, it was really upsetting to see all that talent being overlooked.

On Their Image

How conscious are you of the Carpenters' public image? Does it matter to you at all?

KC: Oh, we've given it an enormous amount of thought. It started on the wrong foot because it's a brother-sister team. A lot of people, because they did not know how to handle it, ended up trying to throw us into a Steve and Eydie or a Sonny and Cher. They would take our publicity pictures with us cheek to cheek, you know. They were just all wrong.

Being brother and sister, which was again different in this business, it ended up being a kind of goody two-shoes image. And because we came out right in the middle of the hard rock thing, because we didn't dress funny and the fact that we smiled, we ended up with titles like Vitamin-swallowing, Colgate-smiling, bland, Middle America. The fact that we took a shower every day was swooped on as symbolic. I mean, it's all nonsense. I know a lot of people who take a shower every day. I know a lot of people who smile.

In an interview once, somebody asked Richard if he believed in premarital sex and he said yes, and the woman wouldn't print it! We were labeled as don't-do-anything! Just smile, scrub your teeth, take a shower, go to sleep. Mom's apple pie. We're normal! I get up in the morning, eat breakfast in front of the TV, watch game shows.

I don't smoke – if I wanted to smoke I would smoke, I just don't like smoking, not because of my image. I wouldn't kid myself about it. I mean, we're not lushes or anything, we're very into wine!

And reviewers didn't like the fact that anybody clean was successful and the more successful we got the more they attacked our image. They never touched our music. We would get critics reviewing our concerts… they'd review the audience. They'd say how ridiculous that somebody came to see the Carpenters in a tie. What the hell's that got to do with our music? And our capabilities as music makers! It's ridiculous.

We've had shows that we knew were not right, something might have been out of tune. But nine out of ten reviews would either review our clothing or the way the stage looked, by making fun of the fact that we carry a lot of equipment.

We're very dedicated to our business. Our life is our music – creating it. We try to do everything with as much perfection as we can. We have certain beliefs, certain loyalties to ways of doing things. You know, it's just nice to be treated the way you are, just like two human beings.

On Hard Rock

Did your criticism in the Melody Maker *of Mott the Hoople represent a hatred of rock or what it stands for?*

KC: No. I love hard rock – or some of it. There's a lot of it I don't like, but then there's a lot of soft rock I don't like. I really don't know what made me say that about Mott the Hoople and after I'd said it I could have died. It got to be a standard joke in the business because we're so different, Mott the Hoople and the Carpenters. It was one of those things you regret saying. To take in all of hard rock – absolutely not.

It's like somebody saying to us, if you like it why don't you do it? That makes about as much sense as Grand Funk doing "Close To You." We're all good at what we do, and I think it would be an insult to hard rock if we did it, because we're not hard rock people. I may not like everything, but if it's good, I've gotta say, "Hey, that's good, but it just doesn't appeal to me." Not "because I don't like it, it stinks." That's not very bright. I apologize to Mott.

On Her Illness

KC: All my strength is not back yet and that alone gets me upset. I'm not used to being slower than I normally am. Being idle is annoying because I never have been, from working on the road to coming into town and going right into the studio.

We haven't had a vacation the whole time we've been in the business. Until in the middle of the *Horizon* album. I went away for four days and I didn't know what to do with myself. Richard and I have never had a vacation. And it's stupid for the two of us to let it get carried to that amount of work and it turned out to be harmful to me. It's going to be a whole learning process for me to do things in a different way... to really seriously calm down and do things at a slower pace, because I'm very regimented. I cannot stand to be late.

I go to bed at night with a pad by the bed and the minute I lie down it's the only quiet time of the day. My mind starts going, "This has gotta be done, that's gotta be done, you've gotta call this." Then I find myself with a flashlight in bed writing down about 50 things that have to be done by 10 o'clock next morning. It's not the best way to be. It's better to hang loose, but I'm just not that type of person.

"Stop worrying," they say. That's a riot. You never calm down recording an album. You would get to 4:00 or 5:00 in the morning, couple of hours sleep and be back in the studio by noon. It's going, going, go.

Richard's creativity was definitely cut back because of our ridiculous schedule. We got to a point where he was not interested in going to the studio and he hadn't written for a while. He was totally exhausted. When I saw that, that upset me. And I said, well we gotta take some time off, so we cancel a tour and end up in a studio. He said no, he doesn't want to do that, so the next thing we'd know there'd be a TV show booked or something, so we were never alone to get any proper kind of rest, you know. He didn't want it.

We were in the middle of a song for the new album. I had been singing straight for three or four years without a break and I finally got so wiped out. I got sores on my vocal cords and my doctor said, "I don't want you to sing for a month." I said, "What do you mean not sing for a month? I'm in the middle of an album." I was home for two days then I was back in the studio.

In Defense Of Richard

KC: You know, there's so much in Richard, just so much that hasn't even been touched. He's so talented it just makes me weep that everybody just walks right by him. They never give him any credit but he does everything. He's the brains behind it. And yet I get cracks like, "Well what does the brother do?" Or you know, I get the impression that it's really nice that I've brought my brother on the road.

Look what he's produced. There are 16 gold records. He's produced one of the most successful acts in the world and nobody gives him any credit. He never gets referred to as a producer, or as an arranger, and they walk right by him as a writer. Richard and John Bettis are terribly overlooked as writers.

I really get upset for him because he's so good and he never opens his mouth. You know, he just sits back and because I'm the lead singer I get all the credit. They think I did it and all I do is sing. He's the one that does all the work. There isn't anything I wouldn't do for him to give him the perfection that we both want.

How long do you like to live with a song before you actually put it on record? Do you need to get inside a lyric or can you go cold into a studio?

KC: One of the things you learn, working with Richard, is to be able to do anything, any time, and because he knows me so well, he knows I can do it. I recorded "I Can Dream Can't I" and I didn't know how the damn thing went, and I kept saying, "Rich, you gotta let me know how this tune goes."

He wanted to record it live with a 40-piece orchestra. I didn't even know how the song went and he said, "Oh I'll give you a tape, I'll give you a tape." And a month went by and I never got a tape and finally I got it. I was listening to it on a Thursday driving in on the freeway and he wanted to record it Friday morning! He never knows what he wants until it's time to do it and he'll hand me over a lyric sheet.

We had trouble on the last album. We were both so tired, so we came home from a five-week tour on a Monday at 12 o'clock and went in that night to record and worked all night. Many days like that. And on my parents' 40th wedding anniversary we worked all day, ran to the anniversary dinner and then went back to the studio at 1:00 in the morning to cut the two things at the beginning and the end of the album, "Aurora" and "Eventide."

Richard made *Horizon* in the worse state I've ever seen him in. I mean, we had got to a point where we didn't want to go to a studio. It was work, because we were so exhausted and we've never had that. We've always been, "Hey, I can't wait to get into the studio," but that last album just drained everything, every drop of blood out of us.

When it was done, we weren't glad it was done; we were upset with the way it turned out. Richard can work unbelievable hours, but this last time it was getting to us. But now it's gotta change. The two of us can't go on like that. The way that things have happened in the last six months, we're just fed up with being treated like two things that the blood spurts out of.

RICHARD: WE'RE NO ANGELS!
On Karen's Voice

Are you ever critical of Karen's work?

Richard Carpenter: We never get too heavy, because to me Karen sings so well that there's good and then there's better. There's nights when she'll play dumb all over the place and she says, "my God, was I awful tonight," because it's her ear.

On top of being at the front of the show and doing all the lead singing, she's listening to every note that's being played by Tony, Bob or me or whatever and she hears every mistake. And she'll say: "My God what was the mistake in this song? Why did you make a mistake in that song? What happened to you here?"

Would she be right?

RC: Yes, always, but the same thing will happen in the opposite direction; Karen will over-inflect this song or move too much backward and forward, or something. I mean it's not something that happens every night, don't you get me wrong. But we do have mistakes… problems.

Do you have disagreements on music or do you have complete empathy on music?

RC: Mostly it's together. Karen did not care for "Superstar" at first. I respected her view, but it's about the best thing for her that's ever been written. So I had to persuade her for about a week. I figured, if she's not into it, we won't do it. But the more I listened to it, the more I got into it, and I said, "Karen, for me, PLEASE do this one!" And by the time it was finished she said, "I had no idea it was gonna sound like this," because I heard the arrangement and all the "ooh baby's" in the back, the oboe and the harp and the strings. She ended up liking it.

There aren't many out of all the tunes we did that she was against, but there are a couple and "Superstar" is one and "Solitaire" is the other. She never liked "Solitaire" at all and it really turned out that she, as far as the commercial ear goes, was right. It's the worst selling single we've had since "Ticket To Ride." So she may, commercially, have been right on that one – not may have, she *was*.

So she's right, but most of the time we agree. Most everything I pick out she loves. I mean, I can hear something and say, "Hey, Karen's gonna like this." There's one I wanted to do for a year and a half, a song off Elton John's *Empty Sky* album, "Sky Line Pigeon." Love it. Can't get Karen to do it. She won't do it. But I can hear it and maybe someday we'll do it. She may be right, in that the bulk of our fans might not understand the lyrics. They are subtle lyrics.

So far, all our stuff has been direct. Fans are difficult. When we came out in *Melody Maker* with a thing about Mott the Hoople we had people quit the fan club. They just said "I'm never gonna buy another album by the Carpenters because of what they said about Mott the Hoople." So who knows whether the bulk of the people would or would not understand the lyrics of "Sky Line Pigeon"?

On Their Image

Do you think your success is partly due to the renunciation of heavy rock or even acid rock? Do you think, had you come along in 1967, you would have flopped?

RC: No, because it's just a whole different audience – one's rock, the other's pop. In 1968 Herb Alpert comes out with a Bacharach/David composition, "This Guy's In Love With You," which could easily have been "Close To You." Went to number one, sold a million and a half copies. It was pop as opposed to rock. "Close To You" could have been a hit in 1954!

And you know, Marty Balin wrote a love song on the Jefferson Airplane's *Surrealistic Pillow* album called "Today" – "Today I feel like giving you more than before." Gorgeous! That's nothing but a love song. Right smack in the middle of the acid rock movement, the premier acid rock song was a love song! And with us, our type of music, especially "Close To You," could have been a hit in 1940, 1950, 1960 – it could have happened any time for us. But it happened in the seventies – beginning of a new decade, decline of acid rock.

People are disgusted with this whole thing of drugs and long hair and although we, the Carpenters, are not claiming anything, a whole lot of people used it for *their* stand! They take "Close To You" and say: "Aha – THAT'S for the people who believe in apple pie! THAT'S for the people who believe in the American flag! THAT'S for the average middle-class American person and his station wagon. The Carpenters stand for that and I'm taking them to my bosom" and BOOM – we get tagged with that label. Well, I just don't believe in that. You try to tell those people that I have every Zappa record, every Mothers record, every Beatles record… that I disagreed with Art Linkletter (TV commentator) when he blamed the Beatles for the death of his daughter.

I got so upset when this whole "squeaky-clean" thing was tagged onto us. I never thought about *standing* for anything! I mean, I realize Presley came along and you can argue whether he filled a void when James Dean was killed, but he stood for something. Rebellious teenagers, and all that.

So our music is just what we do. I mean, I love many different styles of music. I'm a big Zappa fan, been into the Mothers of Invention ever since *Freak Out*, but that doesn't mean just because you understand what he's saying in his lyrics and can get into his avant garde arrangements that you can do it yourself. So we do what we can do. But that doesn't mean we are doing music as a statement of what we believe in, as far as lifestyle goes.

Shopping for furniture on a Saturday or apple pie or whatever – that's how we're bracketed. It's NONSENSE! I look back at some of the pictures, and people didn't know how to deal with a brother and sister act. There's never been one since Fred and Adele Astaire! So they stuck our heads together and said, "Put your cheeks against each other and smile!" And we *did* it! Karen was 19, I was 21. "Put your cheeks together. No, closer! Put your arms around her, smile!" And we did it! So really, how can you blame people for the reaction some got?

We were told when you go out to do interviews, "Don't say anything adverse about anything. Everything is groovy. Everything is terrific. Don't say anything bad. Don't say you dislike anything. You like everything." And we went along with it. We were young. Six years ago. But it's really not what we are.

What you're not selling to the public, which is what a lot of bands do sell, is a lifestyle and an identifiable image. Are you trying to project something beyond your music? Are you saying to your audience, which is what a lot of rock stars say, "We stand for something"?

RC: No. Just listen to the music, enjoy it, and please buy the albums!

Were you interested at all in the youth culture?

RC: No. I mean, I was Middle America – I mean middle class, housing development, the whole thing. And when I first heard Elvis' music, I didn't know what he looked like.

We had some types on our street who leaned towards the black leather jacket, and got in trouble but they didn't talk to me. Where they may have looked up to Elvis because of what he stood for, all I've ever been into is music.

I heard "Heartbreak Hotel," "I Want You, I Need You, I Love You," "Don't Be Cruel" backed up with "Hound Dog" and liked it immediately because of the music, not because of what Elvis stood for. Same with the Beatles. I had to order a Beatles record which I heard on radio station KRLA, which at the time was the number one station in California. In August of '63 they played "From Me To You", which got absolutely no response at all, and I loved it. It excited me. Everything about it was new.

I went to the record store and I said I want a copy of "From Me To You" by the Beatles, and they laughed at me. "The Beatles, there's no group called the Beatles." I said "No, I heard it on KRLA, it's called 'From Me To You' by the Beatles." They look it up. "You're right. Well we don't have it in stock, we'll order it for you." They released it later as the flip of "Please, Please Me", and it got well known. The copy I've got is a collector's item. It was on VJ Records and very, very few of them were made, because it was backed with "Thank You Girl."

I've always made a practice of looking at who wrote what. So I looked at the Beatle thing, saw Lennon/McCartney, looked at the flip, saw Lennon/McCartney – figured they were a duo.

Later I saw a picture in a magazine which said "The Hot Beatles," and I thought "wow, different looking" and there were four of them. FOUR of them? What? You didn't put together a group with a drummer and rhythm guitarist. You didn't think about it!

But anyway, I kept checking to see if any albums were put out, couldn't find anything on the Beatles until six months later, all of a sudden, and "I Want To Hold Your Hand" and boom, the Beatles. But to me it was always their music. Only their music. I never felt them representing anything. I was never into the youth rebellion. That's why it hurt me to be put down and classified into the reverse category. People who immediately took

115

to us were the enemy. They were against us. There're certain groups I don't care for, but that doesn't mean just because somebody's on hard rock, that I don't like them.

Art Linkletter was a fool to come out with that when his daughter died. I think it was right during the time that *Sgt. Pepper* was popular and he came out and said "My daughter's death was the fault of the Beatles," and since that time he's taken back his statement. You know, it was his daughter that overdosed, man. It wasn't the Beatles. The Beatles didn't come to his daughter and say, "hey, overdose." But, you know people could blame anything on the Beatles. Now they can use the Carpenters to describe a lifestyle if they wish, because there's nothing fresh, like in the sixties.

Young kids are more sophisticated. You've got the Four Seasons, one of my favorite groups, and Neil Sedaka, and many other people from the sixties, all getting hit records in the seventies because the people remember how things were before the energy crisis and before things got so tough.

People are going back to the sixties and fifties because they were times when they were happier, so they're buying music by artists who were famous that day. Standing ovations for Simon and Garfunkel coming back again. So many people wish the Beatles were back together.

I'd love to see the Beatles and Simon and Garfunkel get back together. There's something that happens with these sort of groups, even if one person in the group is the guiding light. But when the stars of the group go on their own it's never the same. David Gates when he left Bread, John Sebastian when he left Lovin' Spoonful, John Phillips when he left the Mamas and the Papas, and so many others. When they were together you say, "Hey man it's really mostly Gates, mostly Sebastian, mostly Phillips." And this gets in their mind, so they leave. But it's a great pity. And as much as I like *There Goes Rhymin' Simon*, to me, Simon hasn't come up with "Bridge Over Troubled Water" since he's been on his own. So there must be something about being together with Garfunkel and as much as I like *Band On The Run* and *Imagine*, not one of the solo Beatles has put out anything that can measure up to *Pepper* or *Abbey Road*.

On The Beatles' Genius

RC: I bought "From Me To You" only for the song. I mean, anything that started the major entering the minor was right there. The melody, the intonation was impeccable.

The guys at that time in southern California were not into the Beatles when they hit. I took my *Meet The Beatles* album to school. I was a senior, and brought it around telling people – the guys. They had a contest on KRLA: Who's more popular the Beach Boys or the Beatles? The Beach Boys won.

I was a big Beach Boys fan – forever – but the Beach Boys won on southern California radio because the guys were so pissed off at their girls going on about the way the Beatles looked and the Beach Boys were singing about 409s and "Little Deuce Coupe" and "Surfin'" and everything they dug. Very Californian. The guys were pissed off at a bunch of weird looking guys from England who could possibly challenge the Beach Boys. Well, I just sat back and listened to them both.

We had some teachers at school who were interested. "The Beatles? I've read a lot about them." And they got the record player out and they played the album right there in the classroom. The guys went "Boo," and the teacher went "Awful!" And I went, "Awful?" Can't you *hear* the chord progressions there? Can't you *hear* how different this is?" I really got upset. And I said, "these guys are gonna be around a hell of a long time." Anybody who can write "From Me To You" and "It Won't Be Long" and "All My Loving," which is a beautiful song with a good line tempo, and "Do You Want To Know A Secret," is gonna be around a hell of a long time. I still get really excited about the Beatles.

Didn't their long hair mean anything to you?

RC: The music. Only the music.

What do you think of the four ex-Beatles as soloists?

RC: My favorite was always McCartney. Well lately he's been getting incredible acclaim for *Venus And Mars*, when I feel he should have gotten it for *Band On The Run*. But at any rate, commercially, he's done better than any of them and it's kind of ironic. Ringo's done next best, I think. The first two albums George did – I mean *All Things Must Pass* and *Living In The Material World* – did real well, but sorta flagged off, and now with "You" he's come back. But Ringo, largely due to the efforts of Richard Perry's commercial ear, Ringo has done real well.

Is commercial success all to you?

RC: No.

But you salute McCartney because he is commercially the most successful. Is that the crucial point to you?

RC: No. No it's not. Having a commercial flair is a talent in itself and people shouldn't be put down for being commercial. Melodically, he is superb. And his arranging and rhythmic mind is incredible.

Six years ago, did you want gold discs and fame and the sort of success you've got now?

RC: Oh, I suppose so. Is it a crime to want to sell a million?

On Karen's Illness

RC: She called me today and now she's got the flu on top of her sickness. Her resistance is so low that she picks up everything that comes along.

She really isn't, at this part of her life, strong. She's just kept up far too tough a schedule for her and really run herself down. She always wanted to show she could do just as good as the guys could and really pushed herself. She would never dream of complaining about work, even if she might've not felt like it. In which case she was prepared to go down and she just took on too much. And she went on this huge diet and lost a lot of weight. Oh, she was working so hard. And when she'd eat it would be salad without dressing and she had everything figured out calorie wise. No starch… nothing except things like fish… and never with a sauce.

Anyhow, we had a really hectic schedule. I knew eventually that she'd run herself down. I kept talking with her – it did no good. We did a tour in April and another in May. It was after the one in April that she was flat on her back for several days.

The doctor told her it would happen – "Start eating!" But diet for Karen really became an obsession. She had to lose more weight and so she got well enough to go out and do the main shows – the summer tour. It really hit the last week in Vegas, and on top of being too thin and not eating enough food to keep up with the schedule, it also lowered her resistance so that a cold would come along and she just could not shake it off.

We are very nervous. Also, she gets upset very easily. She's a very tough girl – very strong. There's strong, physically strong, and a very strong personality – a very tough person. When I say tough I mean resilient and persistent personality. The strength of her personality kept driving her on, saying, "I can do it, I can do it." Now she's even nervous about having made the decision to cancel the British tour. It's troubled her all week.

On Overwork

RC: I've never had so much time off as recently. Now I'm starting to wind down. Before we get home from these tours all I want is to sit and listen to the stereo… do nothing more. Go to restaurants… a little relaxation… something to eat. I like to work on my cars. Cleaning them mostly, instead of having somebody else do it. I find it very relaxing and I haven't had the time. I would be so exhausted from the tour and recording. I wouldn't have any energy to bring myself to do it.

Now I'm myself. I found I have more energy than in years. I've been outdoors, catching up on albums and now I actually want to get to the piano and start playing, both just working with original stuff and also I really want to learn Chopin's single piano concerto.

Our overwork has been the reason why there's been so few songs. I mean, John Bettis and I wrote a lot of songs before the success. Not stuff you release commercial single-wise, but we were at least turning some out – a lot for the albums. Whereas for a while, every song we had written since '72 became a single – I mean, I hear it, write it and release it.

First was "Goodbye To Love" and the next was "Top Of The World". They were written the same day and then nothing for a year. I just couldn't come up with anything. I just didn't want to have to go to the piano. And when I came home, I wanted to sit by myself. The next one was "Yesterday Once More" and the one after that was "Only Yesterday," and then there was one other one we wrote, "Can't Say Goodbye." And then two things on the *Horizon* album.

It was no fun writing between tours. Just real hard work. I mean, that's not really much output. What we did turn out did well, but we were definitely not prolific. We used to write a couple of songs a day when we were both in college and the energy was high. But we became like machines these past few years. Producing and performing… the business decisions and foreign tours…

On Their Impact

Do you want to make an impact on pop music for posterity?

RC: Absolutely. I guess people will remember Karen, more than anything, because of her voice. So recognizable. I feel the original success had a great deal to do with Karen's singing more than my arrangements. But I want us remembered in 50 years as the quality, contemporary music duo.

Arrangements play such an important part, though. Without going on and without being cocky or anything, "Close To You" was written in '63 and was out in '63 and wasn't a hit until '70 and my arrangement on it was quite special. It was my arrangement, but the public never recognized arrangers. Singers get famous, songwriters get famous, of course Bacharach and David, of course Lennon/McCartney. But arrangers don't get famous. Mancini would never have gotten famous as an arranger, even though he's brilliant. Bacharach would never have gotten famous as an arranger, even though he's brilliant as an arranger.

It definitely wouldn't be as a singer that I would be remembered. I am a good background singer – not a solo singer. I sing well for a background singer – in tune and a good lung – but I've got a talent as an arranger and as a producer. I mean, all those songs that were hits – every song we've done – I selected them all.

You are 29 and very rich. How does this affect your planning when you need never write or sing another note?

RC: Well, I don't want to, let's say, retire at 30. I just love making music. When you are insecure, you tend to do more than you know you want to do. But Terry Ellis, our new manager, has redefined our future by saying, "You're gonna be here a long time, and your health is more important and you'll be more creative if you have some rest."

So I think we have a good future now. It's not a secure business… music, and sometimes you start thinking, "My God, what if I only last three years?" They tell you to invest your money, and you make enough, work enough and you can retire at 30. I don't want to retire at 30. I don't care if I have millions of dollars. I could be financially secure for the rest of my life and I wouldn't want to retire at 30. I wanna keep doing what I'm doing.

Ray Coleman, former editor of the British pop music weekly Melody Maker, *authored* The Carpenters: The Untold Story. *He died in 1996 at the age of 59.*

Part Three:
There's A
Kind Of Hush

It's An Overdose
Of Pretty

By Joel McNally
Milwaukee Journal (1976)

You may have noticed that a kind of hush fell over the world recently. It was a wonderful sight to see. Everyone laid down their arms and joined hands as brothers and sisters. The reason for this somewhat monumental world event was the release of the new album by the Carpenters, the ultimate brother and sister. The album is appropriately titled *A Kind Of Hush* (A&M), and at this point it is the odds-on favorite to win the Grammy, the Nobel Peace Prize and the Reader's Digest Sweepstakes.

Why can't more kids these days be like these nice young people? While drug-crazed, libertine musicians are doing the devil's work, Richard and Karen Carpenter have, in their own quiet way, worked to restore faith in such sacred institutions as home, family and Patti Page. Oh, not that they don't have a mischievous streak. They are not old sticks-in-the-mud by any means. They have come up with an absolutely wild, madcap rendition of Wayne King's 1930s hit "Goofus." Talk about flaming youth!

Richard and Karen believe in honoring their father and mother by restoring the Big Band sound to its proper place in the world of music. Oh sure, they take a lot of abuse for it. Rock critics compare them with Mickey and Minnie Mouse. That's grossly unfair. Karen does not have skinny black legs and knobby knees. And Richard does not have big, black ears. Pillars of characters and virtue they are, the Carpenters remain utterly impervious to such vicious attacks. All they ask is that they be able to make their simple music. And sell 30 million singles and albums.

The selections on their new album are an interesting collection of period pieces from a variety of periods. They aren't living entirely in the '30s, you know. They have such modern, with-it material as Neil Sedaka's "Breaking Up Is Hard To Do." Actually, it is sort of interesting that Sedaka is still included because, in fact, they didn't find breaking up with him hard at all. Last year they fired Sedaka from opening their Las Vegas act because he got

123

confused about who the star of the show was. It was the first time in recorded history that the Carpenters have been heard to utter a curse – even if it was only "Grimy Gumdrops."

The title song, "There's A Kind Of Hush (All Over The World)," was first immortalized by another extremely hip group, the legendary Herman's Hermits. Many of the other songs are perfectly pretty. That is the problem. With things like their single, "I Need To Be In Love," "Sandy" and "I Have You," Karen's pale white vocals and Richard's overly flawless arrangements make one pretty much as pretty as another – and not terribly distinctive. Even so, one song, "One More Time," stands out as a particularly fine song. The arrangement is simple and Karen's voice and Richard's piano don't get buried under layers of oboes.

There is really nothing wrong with someone who has an appreciation for the more elaborate musical forms of the past. After all, they could be into a lot worse things. Like playing the spoons or running their fingers around the rims of water glasses.

Karen Carpenter:
Nothing To Hide Behind

By Charlie Tuna
Interview Transcript (1976)

Karen Carpenter and I first talked on the phone in 1972. I interviewed her for a radio special on love songs that I was producing at the time. Many more interviews followed after that, including an annual event when I would call her on the air on the morning of her birthday just to wish her "Happy Birthday" and catch up on her latest projects with Richard. Then in 1976 I invited her to come down to the station to "just sit and talk" for an interview that I would play back on the air later that month. She came alone (no record company or public relations people were with her), and she relaxed and talked with me, and seemed to really enjoy herself. What follows are excerpts from that interview, taped October 8, 1976.

What's the TV special? What's the center theme going to be on this?

Well, I think we're just going to call it "The Carpenters First Television Special." [*Laughs*]

Has it been more than you anticipated, as far as work and hours?

Oh! It was an absolute kick to do! We worked on it for a long time. Knock on wood, I really think it came out great, and it was so much fun. I mean, it's a lot of hours. It really is. But that's really fun.

You had some nice guest stars to help you out...

Oh yes we sure did! A good friend of ours, John Denver... and Victor Borge, who is absolutely out of his mind! He's nuts, and just an absolute pleasure to work with, as is John. It was really a lot of fun.

There was a recent People magazine article, which talked about... you've got a condominium you're building?

The condominium is the one I am building in Century City. In fact, it's pretty close to being done. I bought it about two years ago. What I did

127

was take two complete apartments and gut 'em and started brand new. I've got 3,000 or 3,100 square feet of just one big condominium. It's something I've wanted to do for a while.

What does your taste run to, as far as decorating?

Well, we've nicknamed it "contemporary/country/French," which doesn't make any sense at all! It's odd, because I like country, yet I don't like antiques. Certain antiques I like, but I don't get into antique furniture. I like big, fluffy couches.

When I first met with my decorator, John Cottrell, he said, "Well what do you like," and I said, "You better sit down." I explained to him I want it to look classy, in a funky kind of way. I want it to be top-notch, top class, yet I want people to feel like they can put their feet up on anything. He sat down and said "oh dear…" But he's doing a really great job and I've got a combination of a lot of different things. A country kitchen, and on the other hand I've got Lucite and chrome. It's really going to be nice.

As far as the Carpenters' image, I get the impression that that's kind of how you would like the American public to view you, rather than just a placid exterior and not really any funky stuff to it.

Yeah. There's so much that Rich and I like that a lot of times people don't or haven't had the chance to see. But it seemed from Day One we were accidentally plastered with a certain type of an image…

It was very middle-of-the road, I guess, from the beginning.

Well, I don't mind that so much because we're just kind of normal. But as far as certain headlines reading all I do is drink milk and eat cookies… that's not really fair, you know?

Richard, I think, had the classic comment. He had said you make Pat Boone look dirty.

Yeah! [*Laughs*] We're normal. We like to do a lot of different things, and that's what we'd like people to see. We just like to have a lot of fun.

The music during the middle '70s, actually with the advent of "Close To You," began to take on a different trend, though. It seemed people almost considered cocktail rock the "in" thing to do, if that's what the label is that you'd apply to it. And you sort of set a trend for what became a taste as far as music in America.

It was funny because when "Close To You" hit was July 22, 1970. Not that I remember dates… [*Laughs*]

What hour was it?

I think it was, let me see… when *Billboard* comes… about four o'clock in the afternoon, actually… But "Close To You" was (number) one and the next week "Make It With You" by Bread went number one. About the same time, James Taylor was hitting with "Fire And Rain," and right after that I think Carole King hit with "It's Too Late." We named it contemporary pop. [*Laughs*] And then all of a sudden the trend was changing and it stuck. Until about a year-and-a-half ago, and then all of a sudden it changed back around. It's not quite as strong right now, but I have a feeling it's going to come back. I hope it does.

There's a tremendous surge of nostalgia that's happened over the last couple of years and you've gotten into it yourself with some of the hits.

When we went with "Postman" we didn't do that to get into the nostalgia thing. That was something Richard always wanted to cut for some strange reason. He said, "I love 'Please Mr. Postman.'" And I said "What?" And it's a great song! It has got four chord changes, but what you can do with them… I had more fun cutting that record. That and "Goofus." That's forty years old, you know. Gus Kahn wrote it. I thought that might do something and it never really caught on, which I was kind of disappointed about, because it's such a good song. It's a fun kind of thing, you know?

I think since I have known you the past couple of years, you've always had that urge to do "Goofus."

I *really* love it. And like with "I Can Dream Can't I" – something like that. There are so many things you can do. In the whole nostalgia thing we cut the *Now & Then* album, but we never released anything other than "Yesterday Once More." One day we were driving on the freeway and it was right in the middle of everybody releasing oldies. And Rich said, "You know, nobody's ever written anything about the surge coming back." I could see the head lighting up, right before we got off at Highland. And that was it. Five minutes later out came the tune. But we could have pulled "End Of The World," "Johnny Angel," but we never did because he didn't want to get into that. We left them on the album as a whole, which is still one of my favorite albums. That album was more fun to cut. We couldn't get anything done, we were laughing so hard.

I read that you originally started out playing the drums before you even started singing.

It happened pretty close. All I ever heard, and this is the honest-to-god truth, is "girls don't play drums." That is such an overused line, but I started anyway. I picked up a pair of sticks. It was the most natural feeling thing I've ever done and then... that was it. A week later I asked my mom and dad for a set of Ludwig drums. I was never more at home on a set of drums and within six months I was playing with Rich and in another couple of months we won the Hollywood Bowl Battle of the Bands in '66. I sung and played kind of at the same time because we started getting gigs on the weekend and they needed somebody to sing. So Richard said, "Well, sing 'Yesterday'." And then I'd do "Ebb Tide," you know, and all that stuff. But I never stopped playing! I did everything at once.

That's another thing we think about... "Girls don't play drums," but to sing and play drums at the same time is even more difficult.

It was the most *comfortable* thing, and I played the entire show for two years. We were out on the road for two years before Richard finally said, "You've got to get up." We had four or five gold records. We were way into "Superstar" before I finally had to get up. Petrified. You have no idea. The fear. There was nothing to hold onto...

No security blanket.

Nothing to hide behind... My drums... by this time I had so many of them all you could see were my bangs. You couldn't see the mouth, you couldn't see the hands, you couldn't see anything. So we're out on the road and we're doing all the hits and the dummy is buried behind a full set of drums. [*Laughs*] So finally I started getting up.

Was it awkward, because suddenly you didn't have anything to do with your hands?

Oh sure. It took a little while, but now I can't stand still with everywhere I want to run. Now we have incorporated into the show an entire seven or eight-minute drum spectacular. It is just drums. I don't sing a note. We end up with twenty-three drums on the stage, which is something you will also see on the special. I love to play. I *really* do. And I love to sing, but I wouldn't want to give either one of them up.

Who were the people that made the impressions on Karen Carpenter? The style that you have...

Well, I don't think anybody particularly influenced my vocal style. It just kind of happened, because I don't really style myself after anybody. When I opened my mouth it came out and that was it. [Laughs] But as for liking different vocalists, there are just a million of them. Harry Nilsson floors me. This could go on for days. I love the Beatles, the Beach Boys, James Taylor, Dionne Warwick, Dusty Springfield, Ella Fitzgerald... All different types, but I never really copied anybody because, like I said, when I started to sing it just kind of developed. I don't know where it came from, to tell you the truth.

Who makes the decisions? Or is it a mutual decision...

It's pretty much mutual, because another lucky thing is that we think identically on 99% of the things. We very seldom disagree. If there is something that comes up we talk it out. And if it gets down to who's going to make the decision, if it's a musical decision, he'll make it. But I can't even remember when there was that kind of decision that we disagreed on. Oh... yes I do! "Superstar," which, when I think back on it I can't imagine how, but I had heard the tune originally on Joe Cocker's *Mad Dogs And Englishmen*. And then we heard it again on "The Tonight Show" when Bette Midler did it. She did it as a torch song. Richard came running up the stairs and said, "I've found *the tune*," and I heard it and I said, "That's nice." And he said, "NICE?" But he heard the whole record in his head, needless to say. It didn't knock me out until I recorded it, at which time it just blew me over. But that was the only question I ever had.

Somebody said you weren't that enamored with "Solitaire" either. I guess it was an initial impact.

I do stand corrected. I think I heard that the first time in England. I think the versions that I had heard didn't knock me out. I do like the song. It's not my favorite.

That's a diplomatic way...

But it's a beautiful song and Richard produced the hell out of it, he really did. And I like doing it, but there's others that I am more fond of. I think my favorite today is "I Need To Be In Love." That really upsets me when I hear it.

I've had so many ladies on the phone call me and say "That is my song." So many have the empathy…

It really hits me right at home. Certain nights on the stage it really upsets me. I sing it and I'm almost putting myself into tears. It's so personal because John Bettis, our lyricist, wrote that. When Rich heard the title he said "Oh my God, that's beautiful!" John, Richard and I are kind of sitting in the same boat. We're all looking.

You've always been portrayed as loners.

Well, we're not loners, we're just looking for somebody to share our life with and we haven't been lucky enough to find it yet. That's really the easiest way to say it.

What are the requirements you're looking for today, Karen?

Well, I have my list here, but I'll have to stand just in case it hits the floor! Again, John thinks exactly the way we do. That's why when he wrote the lyrics to that thing I was just flabbergasted. The first verse of that when it says "The hardest thing I've ever done is keep believing there's someone in this crazy world for me… The way that people come and go through temporary lives, my chance could come and I might never know…" And I said, "Oh my GOD!" You know, it's so true! It's very hard in the position that we are in, and I know other performers, if they hear what I am talking about, are probably thinking, "Oh yes," not only to meet people but to find somebody that's real.

You have to question their motives a little bit… if they're attracted to you simply because you're a star…

It's a terrible thing to say, but it's kind of true. And it's hard because we're constantly around somewhat of the same circle of people. I find sometimes with guys, a lot of them don't know what to expect. Some of them get upset if we walk into a restaurant and they recognize me and don't recognize him, which puts me away because I don't like to hurt people. A lot of times they don't know how to act. They freeze. I'm saying, "What are you freezing for? It's only me." But they don't realize a lot of times that we're just human, and it's kind of a difficult position to be in. We're always looking for just somebody nice… somebody that's real and has a way with them that's going to make me happy for the rest of my life.

Do you see the business, a broad spectrum of entertainment, as being a problem of having a marriage with somebody?

Not if it's somebody that understands, see. That's a definite problem in itself. It's rough because you spend a lot of time on the road. Obviously I would want to cut down on the work, but you don't have to get married and sit in the house. I couldn't. There's no way I would ever stop singing or performing or doing whatever I want to do. But I want to do it with somebody and share it. I want somebody to share my *joy* with! At the same time, whoever it is I find, I want them to be able to feel the same way... to share *their* accomplishments. There's a lot to do in this world.

What really entertains Karen Carpenter or puts you on your high for a day?

I'll tell you one thing, that I couldn't have said a year ago, is being healthy again. When I got sick it scared the hell out of me. I said, "Whoa!" Right down to the old eighty-nine pounds there. That made me stop and think. It really did. Now I have a priority list. Certain things that would have upset me a year ago don't anymore. Trivial things don't shake me as much. I enjoy what I do immensely. I love to sing. I love making records... performing. Sooner or later I'd like to look into doing a movie.

I'm having an enormous amount of good times doing my condominium. Most of all, I would like to have some more time to be just with my friends. Now, if somebody calls up and says, "Hey, you want to go out?" I say, "Yes, July 6th is free. Not this July 6th, *next* July 6th!" They say, "Well when are you leaving?" "Tomorrow morning." "When are you coming back?" "Oh, I'll be back in about six weeks." It's really rough. You say, "Well listen, I'll call you from Germany... if I can get a line." It's hard because every time you set something up you leave.

What about the mail you get? I was curious because I think you tried to set the record somewhat straight with the People magazine article, and now with the special coming up. Did the mail change, as far as the letters and fan mail you would get, or calls, after that article? Was there a different element that suddenly surfaced?

Um... I wouldn't say too much. There were some people that took the article totally wrong. I find that one of the problems that we faced with that article was that certain people just wouldn't accept that we *are* human. And I find that saddening. We are, by no means, I repeat, trying to put down what we are, because I am not ashamed of what I am and neither is Richard. But the fact that he might smoke a cigarette is not an immoral act. It's just not fair! We are not *drunks*. We are not dope addicts.

When we said in that article that we would have voted for legalization of marijuana, it does not mean that we smoke the stuff. I wouldn't know it if I tripped over it. I have never touched it, I don't care to touch it and it never entered my mind to touch it! But I do feel that this is a free country. People can do what they feel like doing. I got a letter that was accusing me of being a dope addict, which that is absolutely ridiculous! I have never *touched* it, and I really could care less! But I still have a mind of my own and that's what I don't like being deprived of. I do like to be able to speak what I feel. I don't like being cornered and neither does Richard.

As for us putting down the milk and cookies image, that's not fair either. I think we're pretty straight ahead people. We're honest. We try to be very loyal to our fans. We spend 24 hours-a-day worrying about whether our product is good enough. We spend an awful lot of time trying to achieve perfection, as close as we can come, and that's not that easy. It's a full time job and it's by far the foremost thing in both of our minds at all times.

Do you ever get tired of doing those tours, over and over?

Not if you do them right, because I was *real* tired of them about a year ago. And finally my body said, "You're tired dummy, lay down!" But now, things have all changed. We're doing things right. The special is going to be terrific. We go out for maybe two or three weeks at the most at a time. We come home for a couple of weeks, we do something else, and if it's handled properly, which it is being done now, it's fun. You go out just for enough time and when it starts to wear off you come home. If you get tired you come home.

Do you find the trappings of success, that constant demand, the public spotlight that you have to be in... is it something that you regret?

Very seldom. It's one thing when you start out and you say, "I've got to get a hit record." You have *no idea* what is following. You really can't comprehend, but every now and then you're really tired out. You can just want to sit and not be constantly confronted with something. On the whole, I wouldn't trade it for anything in the world. The funny times or the odd moments are when you're overseas, like in Japan or England. It's just unbelievable. You can't go out. You can't go anywhere. The secret ways to get in and out of hotels is very entertaining. You find more ways to do things, but I wouldn't trade it. Never.

How do you recycle yourself to be fresh each evening for a concert when you're performing like that on the road? Is there any mental gymnastics you go through or is it just the audience that does it for you?

It's funny, because people say, "What do you do to warm up and get ready to sing?" Well, I walk about ten steps from dressing room right before they say 'Ladies and Gentlemen, the Carpenters' and then when they *do* say that I walk on and that's it!

How do you unwind? Is it the needlepoint that does it for you?

That helps. I like to listen to music. I like to ride my bicycle, my motor-cycle. [*Laughs*] I love to cook, and as soon as I get into my condominium I'll be doing much more of that.

What's your gourmet recipe? Say you found that special person and you're preparing a dinner that night. Have you got a specialty you'd fix right now?

I love French food. Of course you can't beat a good plate of spaghetti! Oh, there's a whole bunch of things I like to do. It's a toss-up at this point.

We'll wrap it up with the obvious question — you expressed an interest in maybe movies in the future. Any other things you'd like to do? Speaking of movies, which would you see yourself in — dramatic or comedy role?

I'd kind of like to do some kind of a comedy-musical. My favorites have always been... well, Carol Burnett just slays me. I think she's so talented. Lucy, I've been wild about for years... the old "I Love Lucy" shows. Streisand just floors me. She's so good. I would like to do something like that, I really would. But I don't know what's going to pop up or what I would do first. I really couldn't say, but I'd like to do a movie.

We'll look for the television special. That's a start, right?

Yeah! That sure was fun. An enormous amount of fun.

Thank you Karen Carpenter.

Thank you.

Charlie Tuna has worked as morning drive personality for more sta-tions and formats than anyone in Los Angeles radio history: Top 40, AC, Hot AC, Oldies, Talk, Sports Talk and Country. In 1990, the Hollywood Chamber of Commerce honored Charlie with his own star on the Hollywood Walk of Fame.

Carpenters über alles!

By Ray Coleman
Melody Maker **(1976)**

There's a moment in the astonishing new Carpenters stage show in which Karen and Richard hold hands. During their classic hit "We've Only Just Begun," they pretend for a split second to be lovers, looking straight into each other's eyes. A rarely-seen moment of near passion from a brother-sister act not noted for warmth, in spite of the romantic beauty of their songs.

Even the most ardent Carpenters fan might be forgiven a groan of embarrassment. There they are now, compounding the appalling Mickey Mouse, "squeaky clean, apple pie" image which has plagued them for two years.

Speaking as a fully paid-up Carpenters music follower for six years, I felt the flesh creep uncomfortably at the sight of grown-up brother and sister acting out this slightly incestuous scene as just "part of the act." But that's precisely what it is. "We've never been a touching or kissing family. We were not raised that way," Richard says.

"And now, when we're thinking about it, it seems natural and normal." says Karen. People who came to see the show, close friends and managers, said it was ridiculous that we didn't touch each other throughout," says Richard. "So we put it in."

Right now, after a couple of inferior albums and a failed battle to wipe out their antiseptic image, they are at a crossroads, prepared to be adventurous, even dangerous.

Karen says holding hands felt uneasy for a while. Richard, too, fought off the idea on the grounds that they were "not in love that way." And then, in the context of a violent change in their stage act, they agreed to get closer to each other.

This strange episode in the evolution of the Carpenters, the band that has made it almost hip to like middle of the road music, characterizes as well as anything the convolutions of their appearances, both public and private.

They are currently at a tricky stage of their career. Wealth has been achieved, musical credibility established. Yet there's this nagging feeling that they are marking time. And with Karen's serious illness of last year still lingering as a memory, there seems a desperate need to plow into a new direction, make some noise, and raise the roof!

And so it came to pass that the Carpenters' caravan of 20 rattled into Germany last week for a pre-British whistle-stop tour to show off their daring 1976 look. And to be sure, the old act has been shaken, rattled and rolled into a frantic production routine which projects the Carpenters as you've never seen them before – a show reversing the emphasis on Karen's voice into a slick two-hour whizzo of entertainment.

Richard no longer sits sternly at the piano – he roars on stage on a motorcycle at one point during a spoof of the fifties. And Karen has abandoned that forlorn stance in a sad little red dress which so helped to dent their reputation last time. Now she tears at three sets of drums and a battery of congas, looks kookie in jeans, changes from sharp culotte suit to beautiful ball gown, and acts neatly while dressed as a fifties tart during the motor-bike sequence.

It's an amazing transformation, conceived because the producer, Joe Layton (who worked similarly devastating tricks for Diana Ross' show), believes the Carpenters' millions of record buyers want to see Richard and Karen DO something beyond stand up there and sing. After all, he reasons, fans have the records at home. Who needs a replica of that?

The positive view of the mind-boggling new Carpenters stage show would be that they have planted the kiss of life on a two-year-old corpse and that their audacity has won. Their 1974 show was boring. The 1976 show is over-ambitious.

The uncharitable could say that they have snatched catastrophe from the jaws of disaster. The truth lies somewhere between those extremes. Like it or not, the new show forces a reaction. Nobody sleeps during this concert. The Carpenters are alive and well – and working hard, as always. They know no other way.

The Carpenters are something special, as their German fans loudly affirmed last week. Like their British dates, there were sell-out concerts all the way across Europe, from the Deutsche Museum in Munich to the Dusseldorf Philipshalle to the Hamburg Congresscentrum.

Richard and Karen are hardly pop stars in the accepted sense (he adopts the classic paranoid stance of wanting to be noticed but resenting intrusion into privacy; Karen is too lacking in visible neuroses to be considered a star). Above all, the Carpenters and their five regular accompanists are musicians. Troupers in the grand tradition. It's not rock 'n' roll, but it is too musically innovative and melodic to be considered crass showbiz. The standard of musicianship is very high. And they do, after all, have the strength of the most delectable female voice in its field since, say, Sarah Vaughan or Peggy Lee.

The Carpenters are important because they are exemplary craftsmen. And they touch people. "In a way," says their quietly canny electric bassist, Danny Woodhams, "Rich and Karen HAVE changed the course of popular music in the past six years.

"It's become respectable for a musician like me to say, 'I play with the Carpenters.' Without them, it would have still been acid rock and Motown. It's a testing time right now, but that track record of work between Richard and John Bettis (lyric-writer) is amazing, and Karen's voice... well, it's just lovely."

Richard, however, seems bothered that when the history of popular music has to be written, the Carpenters will not merit a chapter. "Beatles, Beach Boys, Dylan – they'll get chapters," he said. "Not the Carpenters. They'll bracket us, with a load of others as 'bland,' 'easy listening,' 'middle-road.' We've gotta change all this and it's gonna take time."

Still, he was encouraged by the admiration of artistically lesser breeds. He points out that Alice Cooper had gone on record as admiring the Carpenters, and Karen said, "Kiss like us, you know." She raised her eyebrows in mock disbelief.

"As far back as 1971," said Richard, "I've been concerned that we've not been accepted as well in concert as on record. It's sure not the fault of Karen's voice, because she sings the same anywhere... everywhere... in the studio or on stage, the same. The group's usually been clean and tight. No, some magic was missing.

"For five years now it's been worrying me. I'd get home from shows and say, 'No, we're not getting the same thing going on stage that we do in the studio.' Charisma. That's been missing. Guess we're now trying to graft charisma on to our act.

"There's people who don't sing as well as we do and haven't had our amount of hits who aren't a fraction as well-known as us getting the audiences going. Thus far, we've failed in that direction. And yet, I know we're a good group. Not perfect, but good.

"When you know you're doing a good concert and not pulling in a response from the audience, it's demoralizing. To some extent, its the people. They're an older crowd and they don't go 'Whoooooooohoooo' when we do our hits. On the other hand, the nice part is they don't go talking all the way through the songs, either.

"Well, I'd worry myself sick about all this. I'd go home with Karen after a show and say, for an act that sold so many records that doesn't get something better going on stage, there's something wrong.

"But our manager said, 'don't worry, those people who came to see your concert will be back.' And they came back. We kept selling out.

"So I said, maybe we're just selling records to quiet people! Anyway, it built up in my mind and nagged away. So here we are, with this radical change. Joe, the director of the show, says we've all been playing the role of good musicians too long.

"He says we're too good – people don't want to concentrate on music so much. If they want the Carpenters sound they'll stay home with the stereo. I'm not sure. We'll see on the next tour whether they come back. It's a test."

Karen: "We're hams. We enjoy dressing up and the production. Have we gone over the top? Well, the answer's in the audience; its been received well everywhere so far. Ask me next year."

She's leaving home. Very soon Karen will depart the house she and Richard live in with their parents, and set up her own Los Angeles home. She's 26, Richard 30. They get along well, but Karen feels the need to build a house as some kind of personal statement. Richard has encouraged the move. Together, they scarcely seem to look at each other, yet there's natural bond, and at a Munich press conference last week, answering outstandingly banal questions, they unitedly stonewalled with impressive brevity.

Later that night, when I asked both together to name the other's most irritating characteristic, Richard bridled slightly, while Karen came straight out with it. "He'll always stall when we're due to go in the studio and not let me know the title or nature of the song until we get there.

"I keep saying, for days before, 'What's the song?' And he keeps saying 'Oh, you'll be okay. It's easy for you.' He doesn't let me know what my work is until we get inside the studio. I hate that about him."

Richard thought deeply before being pushed to this reply: "If I'm with a girl Karen doesn't like, she gets in her three cent's worth, and then doesn't leave it at that. And after a while it starts to get on my nerves, and we argue.

It's usually not musical. I wish Karen wouldn't sometimes interfere so much in my personal affairs."

Did Richard interfere with her personal life, or did Karen accept his role as big brother? "Not a lot – sometimes I'll offer a view, but I'd never tell her to date this guy or that. I figure that'd be impertinent. However, Karen seems to see it as her duty to give me advice. I don't like that."

What were their joint worries? "Staying where we are," they answered in unison. "Maintaining. Very difficult in the American pop market," Richard said. "You know, it seems that if you're in country and western and you make a couple of hit singles, you're there for life. Not in pop. We can go down as quickly as we came up if our records stop selling."

And how vital was it to him and Karen to keep on keeping on, achieving massive record sales? More important than their private lives now?

Karen answered that if it came to a choice between privacy and fame, hers would be fame rather than privacy. Her career meant everything to her. "I gotta sing. I love that crowd…"

Richard was more equivocal. "Sometimes I think it wrong that we aren't famous enough in person, considering the millions of records we've sold. Sometimes we are not noticed in the street and that gets to me. Other times, I get hassled in a restaurant and don't like that either."

Yes, he agreed, he wanted it both ways. John Denver belonged to the same management stable as the Carpenters, and Richard couldn't stand the prospect of that lack of private life. On the other hand, he envied Denver the ego satisfaction. In the end, Richard wanted to go to the grave having been regarded primarily as a musician rather than pop star. "You can be a pop star for a week," he said thoughtfully. "I'm gonna be a musician forever."

Talking of death, he wanted to die in his sleep. Karen, too. Both are certain that whatever else they record, the song "We've Only Just Begun" will be their musical epitaph. "Huge though 'Close To You' was," said Karen, "it didn't have the impact of 'Begun,' and no one song has been so associated with an act so much for a long, long time as that with us."

Richard said college music students were even writing essays on the theme of that one song, and Richard and Karen were consistently being questioned about it. "Yep, that's the song that's going to remain with us and if you ask me what song I'll take to the grave, that's the one."

If the Carpenters are refreshingly uncloying when they sit together, they lead different lives, and have separate worldly views when they're apart. In

Germany, apart from a chilling trip together to Dachau concentration camp and a visit to a Charles Aznavour concert, they went largely separate ways, partly because Richard has brought to Europe his girlfriend Mary Pickford.

During the day, both keep an extremely low profile, the very opposite of the traditional boisterous traveling circus which so many seven-piece acts offer as a sideshow to the passing observer.

Richard, a piano fanatic, made a point of checking out the Steinway manufacturing house because he believed pianos made in Germany were of better quality than those made elsewhere. Karen did a sharp look around Dusseldorf to establish that it was a vital city. They have separate identities and go their own ways.

But in the evening she's the singer in the band. While the more brooding Richard is a razor-sharp, gifted musician confronting his gaunt and wasted look with musical masterpieces, Karen's vocals are so stunningly warm as to defy comparison. The lady seems incapable of singing out of tune.

Their band is the same as that which came for the plastic show which graced our stages in 1974, and their unashamed loyalty to Richard and Karen is something they freely admit: Danny Woodhams (electric bass, vocals), Bob Messenger (keyboards, bass, flute and tenor sax), Doug Strawn (vocals, keyboards and electric clarinet), Cubby O'Brien (drums) and the dazzling guitarist Tony Peluso, whose love of the Carpenters was such that he turned down an offer from Paul McCartney to join Wings. Peluso's legendary solo on "Goodbye To Love" is now more heavily into feedback, but its melodic strength is intact, and it's still a killing showstopper.

The new show begins with an immaculately suited Richard walking out to bow to the audience… a bow that emphasizes his great height. When Karen emerges for a jazzed-up version of "There's A Kind Of Hush," and "Top Of The World," looking more attractive than in recent years and dressed in a culotte suit, it's immediately apparent that they've acquired a presence missing in any show they've done before.

And when strings sweep them into the glorious ballad "I Need To Be In Love," the hallmark of the Carpenters' beauty – haunting melody plus tasteful arrangement plus that voice – is rammed home with some force. Karen sings that line: "It took a while for me to learn that nothing comes for free/the price I've paid is high enough for me" with a conviction that could strike a chord in many a broken heart, so meaningful is her voice.

There follows a "City Slickers" segment which marks the ruination of "Close To You" as a song – it's speeded up to two or three times its recorded tempo, with lead vocal by Richard and the rest of the band spoofing it up with kazoos and hooters a-la Temperance Seven.

It's awful, but Karen reappears quickly enough to repair the damage. She has changed dresses again, and looks splendid (she has recently acquired the services of the same clothes designer as Olivia Newton-John, one of Karen's friends).

"Sing" calls for audience involvement, Karen moving among the front rows for a volunteer to join her. (A fundamental mistake, for it diminishes their role as stars who should keep a distance from the audience.)

"Mr. Guder" and the glorious "Yesterday Once More" come before Tony Peluso's breathless spoken introduction of the fifties sketch. This is spirited stuff, with Richard riding a motorcycle on stage, Karen acting the role of his girlfriend with genuine acting flair, band joining in with a doo-wop vocal parody and Karen looking every exaggerated inch the fifties tart, complete with gigantic bouffant wig.

She follows this with a splendid attack on the drums (three kits and congas) during a mini-biographical sketch on the Carpenters' career story, narrated by Richard and Karen alternately. A filmed backdrop provides a good glimpse into their growing-up years.

Richard's piano peaks are scaled with a fine, serious "Warsaw Concerto," before the hits start rolling: "For All We Know," "Ticket To Ride," "Only Yesterday," "Please Mr. Postman," "Superstar," and a wretched encore with two improbable songs for the Carpenters: "Good Vibrations" and – horror of horrors – "Comin' Through The Rye."

There's an air of desperation about the show – but at least it's a positive effort to blitz the audience with something beyond Carpenters music. The big question for their crucial British season, starting this week, is whether they've reversed too far and skated too thinly over their real strengths, the songs. Clearly, they had to do something, and they can't be accused of being stagnant. More than anything, I think the new Carpenters show qualifies them for bravery medals. Less bold stars with 30 million record sales would have sat tight.

And when all's said and done, the Carpenters are not disco and they represent standards. In these often-dark days, they are a beacon of light… a good force in popular music. This week in Britain, they'll send 46,000 people out of the theatres with a happy smile. That's something.

Concert Review: London Palladium, November 25, 1976

Variety (1976)

To say the Carpenters use every conceivable device, from pots and pans to a motorcycle, as part of their impressive new show, in for a week at the London Palladium, is only slight exaggeration.

Just when the large stage seems crammed to overflowing – with Karen Carpenter's four drumkits and nine visible mikes, brother Richard, five band members, assorted keyboards, electric flutes, clarinets, guitars and tape recorders – the backdrop vanishes to reveal a 42-piece orchestra.

Messy as it sounds, this is slick staging by Broadway producer Joe Layton, and the production as a whole is value-for-money entertainment.

The Carpenters, six years on, are in fine form.

From a slightly raised platform, fringed with red streamers like a giant Christmas cake, they provide their own potted discography beneath an assortment of some 60 spotlights.

Razzle-dazzle effect of the act is enhanced when they leave the stage to enlist audience support for a mad arrangement of "Close To You."

A wheel-on percussion table, which boasts pots and pans, klaxon horns, tin whistles, etc., provides a fun number and Karen Carpenter displays boundless energy and flair with her lengthy drum solo.

Endorsing their pro-publicized changed-from-clean image, they launch into a college skit with bobbysox, false busts, a rude song about Sandra Dee and a noisy climax by Richard driving a motorcycle on stage covering the first 10 rows with fumes.

In more serious vein Richard gives a virtuoso piano rendering of the "Warsaw Concerto" backed by the Dick Palombi Orchestra and reflected in a huge suspended mirror.

The femme Carpenter takes her turn with a "studio session" singing a medley of the duo's disk hits such as "Top Of The World" and "For All We

145

Know," etc. She seems to be on stage during the entire show yet somehow manages five costume changes.

The boys in the band have their own highlight with "Goodbye To Love" and an exceptional guitar duet by Tony Peluso and Bob Messenger.

Audience loved it all — seventy-five minutes of entertainment bristling with vitality.

Carpenters' Surprise

By Ed Harrison
Billboard (1977)

Karen and Richard Carpenter may well surprise a lot of people with the release of their new A&M album *Passage*. The duo concedes that it's their most diverse album yet, touching all bases of the musical spectrum from the reggae-sounding "Man Smart, Woman Smarter" to the orchestral "Don't Cry For Me, Argentina" from the rock opera *Evita*.

Says Richard Carpenter: "On this album we let the musicians stretch out more on the solos. We usually build an album from the bass, piano and drums, but are now incorporating brass, percussion and congas. We used more musicians to get a better feel."

The most elaborate undertaking on the album is "On The Balcony Of The Casa Rosada/Don't Cry For Me, Argentina," which includes the services of the entire Los Angeles Philharmonic Orchestra and the Greg Smith Singers. By the time the tracks were ready to be laid down, 162 performers had assembled on the A&M soundstage.

"When we brought in all these pieces we didn't know if it would work," says Richard. "But we wanted to do it in a big way. And we wanted an orchestra which plays all the time rather than studio musicians."

Other tunes covered include such diverse material as Michael Franks' "B'wana She No Home," Klaatu's spacey "Calling Occupants Of Interplanetary Craft" and "I Just Fall In Love Again," another big orchestral production. Other luminaries contributing include Leon Russell on piano, saxophonist Tom Scott and King Errisson on congas.

"Because of the arrangements," says Richard, "there is a more sophisticated sound. I feel that little has actually changed except maybe compared with some of the older albums."

Adds Karen: "When choosing a song, the melody must fit me first, although the lyrics are also important."

Karen, since the past two albums, has ceased playing drums to allow her to concentrate on singing. Richard wanted a stronger sound she says, "and I no longer have the strength." Karen's singing has also taken on an air of

refinement since the earlier albums. "I used to over-sing," says Karen. "I was too loud. I'm able to feel a song now."

Under the guidance of manager Jerry Weintraub, the Carpenters will begin making selective television appearances. They will have their own Christmas special this year and contemplate one or two specials every year. "Jerry got us the TV deals," says Karen. "He's thinking in more long range. Before, we would just record and tour. Now TV is taking up a lot of time."

The Carpenters, however, are shying away from what some call the traps of a possible weekly variety show of their own. "We don't want to over-expose or exhaust ourselves. It would be impossible doing a weekly. If we did, we'd have to sacrifice everything else," says Richard. "TV might cause a brief spurt in album sales, but our own show would have to be done right," he adds.

Both Karen and Richard concede that their somewhat wholesome image has made for "closet Carpenter freaks." "There are a lot of fans who kind of hide the fact they like the Carpenters," says Karen. Nevertheless, they receive stacks of mail from young people thanking them for straightening out their lives and giving encouragement through such songs as "Top Of The World" and "We've Only Just Begun."

"We like appealing to all ages," Karen says. "Everyone from young kids to their grandparents come to our shows."

What lies ahead for the Carpenters? Karen says she would like to do a film musical while Richard is eyeing other acts to produce.

The Carpenters Go Country?

By Nancy Naglin
Country Music (1978)

When I interviewed Karen and Richard Carpenter in 1978, I was struck by Karen's fragility, the impossible and alluring slenderness of her body and, most especially, the translucent quality of her skin. She was an enigmatic personality who welcomed the attention but disclosed personal information with sweet regret – or was it resignation? My curiosity piqued, I tried to get beneath the surface and so asked about her charm bracelet, an odd and clunky piece of jewelry for the '70s. Each charm meant something, a personal milestone. Dutifully enumerating them, she sounded like an emissary from a private world.

I talked about the impact Karen Carpenter had on me with friends. I wanted to describe her peculiar detachment in the article; however, I believed my speculations were inappropriate. Her unnerving ethereal presence haunted me then and over the years. I had never seen anyone starving to death before.

"Sweet, Sweet Smile" by Karen and Richard Carpenter has been on the charts for 15 weeks. After ten years at the top of the squeaky-clean pop music field, after millions of records sold, this is their first country hit. They seem a little surprised and confused. Yes, they are happy with the hit, but don't seem to know what's next.

The Carpenters' childhood hometown – New Haven, Connecticut – with its church spires poking through the drizzle and the gulls huddled in the reeds alongside the railroad tracks – is a long, cold way from sunny Los Angeles. Years of back-to-back touring, inhuman schedules and an obsessive attention to detail, sometimes bordering on the neurotic, have brought them light years away from their humble New England beginnings. But even comfortably at home in their A&M Records office, sister Karen and brother Richard, basking in the glow of their 18 gold records, are sunstroked yet with the sudden success of "Sweet, Sweet Smile" from their *Passage* album.

151

"I knew it was off the wall," says Karen, absolutely mystified by the tune's success. She has just come from an all-night session, putting the finishing touches on a TV special and although exhausted, she is still revved up. "A true workaholic." Richard's word to describe them both.

"Ever since 'Top Of The World' happened with Lynn Anderson, people always ask us how come we didn't have a hit on it in the country field." She turns to brother Rich – partner, arranger and companion – and shrugs. He opens his mouth to answer; she blithely reads his mind.

"It's because we released ours as a pop single after she had the (country) hit. Ever since then we always thought it would be possible but we never did anything." Rich nods in agreement.

The Carpenters, for years the darlings of the squeaky-clean, middle of the road, easy listening sound, with their TV specials and Vegas shows, have wandered across the charts into Opryland and they're not quite sure how it happened.

"We're kind of soft, easy-going country," Richard concedes, groping for the words to properly describe his sound.

"We always try to get one country song on our albums," adds Karen. "Not for any specific purpose, but because we like it. We don't go in and say, 'we've got to record a song that will get on the country charts.' We always just go in with what we like." Then she flashes her famous down-home smile, bright with the reassurance of a flight attendant's welcome.

Although the Carpenters, versatile survivors of a dozen years and almost as many music trends, are bewildered by their tune's success, they are genuinely delighted in finally finding a country audience. In the hard rock days of the late '60s, they nearly got left behind before they really started. Then James Taylor floated in with the easier sound of the '70s, and they felt redeemed. Through it all, the Carpenters have remained a self-sufficient, inward-looking team who select, arrange and produce their music without ever going beyond the family circle. "Yeah, it's always been that way," says Richard. "It seems like if you ask five different people, you get five different answers."

"It was like when we first got started and we were mixing 'Ticket To Ride,'" recalls Karen. "It finally got around to where we were asking so many people that it seemed that the next person we were going to ask was..."

"The security man," says Richard, his voice coming in on top of hers.

If their music now has a country flavor it's because, self-consciously or not, the sound has filtered through Richard's ear. According to Karen, when album time rolls around, Richard goes home with a carload of material and begins "the ever-long search through the piles of things that come in."

"No, I don't write. It's sad, isn't it?" she says brightly, as Rich stares at the floor. "Nothin' ever came out."

By chance, Karen was visiting a friend who played a tape of "Sweet, Sweet Smile," written by singer/songwriter Juice Newton. She brought it home to Rich, and as soon as he heard it, he wanted to add a few things – like a banjo.

"When I hear country, all of it sticks," he says, tilting his head to the side as if he's reading off a sheet of imaginary sheet music. When he was a kid, his father was a big fan of Spade Cooley, and Richard spent hours listening to 10-inch LPs recorded in the early '50s. Cooley's sound was smooth with full brass and reed sections. "Then there was the steel guitar. See, I remembered it," he says tapping the side of his head.

"And it's not like we didn't do country before," explains Karen, mentioning "End Of The World" on the *Now & Then* album (1973) and "(I'm Caught Between) Goodbye And I Love You." Like Kenny Rogers with "Lucille" and Olivia Newton-John, they've crossed into country but whether they have the intention or desire to stay is still in question.

"We were very excited when this thing started," says Karen cautiously, as if still not believing the charts.

"But if we were going to go in and snap out a country single, well, that wouldn't happen at this point," says Richard definitely. "Of course, it would be great if it happened again."

"To this day people ask who I style myself after? Who influenced me and to that I say 'nobody.' But when I first began I sounded very country," says Karen. "You got a country streak in you," she proudly remembers electrical bass guitarist Joe Osborn saying when he recorded their demo tape in his North Hollywood garage back in 1968.

They have discussed going to Nashville. "For the players," says Richard, his eyes gleaming. He's an obsessive-compulsive perfectionist who once flew to Nashville to record exactly two bars of music for the "Desperado" cut on the *Horizon* album. But as much as Nashville studio musicians entice him, he's true to the sound he hears in his head. The only way they'll make a Nashville album is if the album warrants Nashville talent, and judging by the way their albums get put together, when – or if – that happens is anybody's guess.

"It's nice to be able to pick your own stuff, have total control," says Richard. "The thing is, you're responsible for it if it hits or if it flops."

His bottom line is the artistic quality. He started playing piano when he was 12, and knew that one way or another music was his world. Karen "kind of followed him around," starting to sing when she was about 16, and then getting them both kicked out of clubs because she was too young to drink. That led to an early recording career, and both claim that over the years their ears have sharpened. Rich just about shudders remembering the creaking of a closing door that made it on to one of his albums.

Then followed years of hectic touring until Karen collapsed in 1975. "We realized then that we didn't need to run all over the world like maniacs," says Richard, and instead they developed a Vegas act. "If it costs, it costs," says Richard," because it's got to be what I hear."

Since "Sweet, Sweet Smile," there's been talk of the Grand Ole Opry. Karen is especially intrigued by the possibility of a new audience. There are the TV specials and the Vegas show that needs to be overhauled, but she's looking for something new, even considering TV roles.

"We pride ourselves in being trendsetters for the easier listening sound." She speaks slowly, as if oppressed with the role. "When we started we were knocked for being dressed cleanly, for taking a bath. We were titled sweet and clean," and when she says, "Goody four shoes," Richard laughs and shakes his head.

Now he wants to produce other artists. Both of them, too, would like to marry and set up private lives. "But schedules make it difficult to meet people and date," says Karen wistfully. "We always worked together," she says, looking back over eight albums, her hand resting beneath a gold charm in the shape of a record, a Christmas gift from a grateful record company. "I'm hoping – but I – neither one of us – have found anybody we'd want to get married to. We have so much to give and we've accomplished a lot on our own. It would be nice to share it with somebody. At this point, we're just sharing it with each other."

"The group, too, has been together for 10 years," says Richard about the guys in the band who are like an extended family.

And if they cut another surprise country hit or if they took up the invitation to the Grand Ole Opry? "We'd have to go just the way we are," says Richard unhesitatingly. And doing things in their own sweet time, living like cactus in the desert of L.A., off their own juices, the Carpenters may be just a little more country than they think.

Concert Review:
MGM Grand, Las Vegas,
March 7, 1978

Variety (1978)

Richard and Karen Carpenter followed no trend nor succumbed to rock critics' irascible putdowns of their music when they came upon the scene about 10 years ago.

It was the softest of sounds on the contemporary scene lumped under rock 'n' roll, but the Carpenters really made their own kind of sound and music, then and now.

If it was said to be dated then, it is dated now. But it is not. It is directly in the melodic pop mainstream currently enjoying high popularity.

Neither Karen in her singular style and timbre of song projection, nor her brother Richard as the songwriter-performer-leader had or have any deep, emotional, heavy-laden statements or profundities in their music. They are pop tunes, pure and simple, and the audiences at the Grand respond strongly to their messages of entertainment.

The act itself has held on to same format for some time and it's a slick one showcasing the leads as well as the excellent quintet that helped create the indigenous Carpenters sound. A new direction, possibly, could follow or coordinate with their latest spacey record album, but certainly the solid hit parade built up over the years would be a mandatory inclusion.

If Somebody Would Just Let Us Know What The Problem Is…

By Bill Moran

Radio Report (1978)

Since the release of "Ticket To Ride" in 1969, the Carpenters have not missed charting with any single. For the record book, that makes 22 consecutive chart singles. Recently they added a new dimension to their career by breaking country radio with "Sweet, Sweet Smile." In this interview, the Carpenters reflect on their recording career and their problems with Top 40 radio in 1978.

It's been almost 10 years since your first chart record. You've sold millions of records around the world, 30 million in the U.S. alone. Is it still fun?

Karen Carpenter: Yes, very much so. In fact we just returned from Germany about a day ago, so we're kind of just getting readjusted. We went over to do a television show called "Star Parade." It's an hour and a half variety show that is done live six times a year. It goes out to a minimum of 30 million people. It's amazing that at any given time during the hour and a half, it's covered on 56 percent of the TV's in Germany.

Richard Carpenter: The show was even seen in Sweden and in Holland.

KC: It's really wild. ABBA was the only other group that we knew. There were people from everywhere. There was one group from Israel and there were groups from France and England.

Is the international market as big as it's always been for the Carpenters?

KC: Yes, very big. "Calling Occupants Of Interplanetary Craft" was a gigantic hit in Japan, and "Sweet, Sweet Smile" is coming on like gangbusters in Germany. What we really want to do is get our market back in the United States.

Are you saying that Top 40 radio is resisting your music here?

KC: We've been asking ourselves that question for almost three years. For the last three years there has been a definite resistance to our product and I don't know why. We've been doing our best to turn out the finest product we can. Richard keeps changing direction. We've covered practically every aspect that is capable of being put to disc with the exception of classical. We haven't done that yet, but...

"Occupants" was certainly a change of direction, wasn't it?

KC: You could say that, and as far as being timely, it was ahead of the game because we cut that before *Star Wars* hit the market.

Then what's the answer to this dilemma?

KC: It's a very touchy question to us at this point. We just don't know what Top 40 radio is looking for. One minute they say they're looking for a traditional Carpenters record. We give them one of those and they don't want it. They say they want something different, so we give them "Occupants" and they don't want that either. We give them country and Top 40 again resists. If somebody would just let us know what the problem is, then we could take it from there. Everybody has a different answer.

What are some of the answers you're getting and what are some of the Top 40 guys telling you?

KC: We talked to Paul Drew. He said come out with a three-minute record. We did that and nothing happened on Top 40 radio. It's the weirdest damn thing. They just turn it back at us. We're trying. That's what's frustrating.

RC: We've had a change of direction, which I wanted to do anyway. Not a total turn around, but just a couple of things were different. Then they said that "Occupants" was just a little too far out. They didn't like the guitar solo in the middle. There was a guitar solo in the middle of "We're All Alone."

I guess it doesn't matter what they say, does it?

RC: Well, you can't have anything over 3:15. So we come out with "Sweet, Sweet Smile" which is three minutes and Top 40 doesn't play it. I think you have to do what you want to do. You have to do something you're most comfortable doing... something that doesn't sound contrived.

Is your image hurting you as far as Top 40?

KC: I couldn't answer that. I'm getting sick and tired of this image thing. What is the matter with a brother and sister team who happen to be the first ones who just record and enjoy life?

Are artists forced to stay in a mold?

RC: There are some that I think have to keep changing and want to change and there are others that I don't think will ever change. I don't think one thing applies to all artists.

Does it get to the point where radio says to an Elton John, a John Denver, and the Carpenters that enough is enough?

RC: The American people are fickle. They go from one extreme to another with an artist. And I think radio wants to cater to them. If an act gets hot then people can't get enough of it. I'm relating your question now to records, artists, and radio.

Like what the Bee Gees are into right now?

RC: I love the Bee Gees. I thought they were turning out great product all along. I was into them starting with "New York Mining Disaster 1941." They went on for years without anything happening. Now it's Bee Gees, Bee Gees, Bee Gees.

Is it almost a burnout problem?

RC: I think that is what is going to happen. It happened with Elton John.

It may have happened to the Carpenters.

RC: I was just going to bring that up. It did happen to us. And the same thing happened to the Captain and Tennille.

Relative to the Carpenters, how do you counter the burnout thing? Was there a saturation of Carpenters product?

RC: It wasn't a matter of too much product. What happened was that our sound was new. We've got a lot of people borrowing the sound. On top of our own records, there were other records coming out. It's about time that people stopped trying to imitate us. This one particular riff is still being used and used and used from the beginning of "Close To You." I still hear it. We set a trend and everybody jumped on it.

Are you looking for outside material?

KC: Sure, all the time.

Were you the first to do "Can't Smile Without You?"

RC: Yeah, we introduced it two years ago. We did the whistling and the whole thing.

In other words, it's all in the timing.

RC: Yes, and Barry Manilow is hot.

Do you feel there is any creativity left in Top 40 radio?

RC: I feel the playlists are a little too tight and the records get played more than they ever did. But there are some nice records out now and some are getting played.

What have your experiences been when you have visited radio stations?

KC: There is so much going on in the recording studio, especially with all the TV things. We spent an awful lot of time on the TV special. That took about three months. Unfortunately, it does not give us much time to visit radio stations.

RC: Karen and I really get off on doing interviews. We enjoy doing them and you can't get away from them.

You mentioned all the time it takes to do TV and personal appearances. Does that take away from the real bread and butter, the making of records? Or, is recording no longer the real bread and butter?

KC: We still feel it is. We don't spend as much time as we would like to in the studio, even though we spend an enormous amount. We haven't really been on the road in a long time. We should go back out. That is an area where we are sorely missed. We feel it's our fault too. You just start to get into a pattern and all of a sudden things start weaving.

Have you ever given any thought to using an outside producer, particularly during the last couple of years?

RC: No.

Karen, have you ever given any thought to doing solo things?

KC: We've thought about it. There were things I've done that were just the lead vocal, songs like "I Just Fall In Love Again," "I Can Dream Can't I," "Sometimes," etc. This brings us back to the fact that we want to get back to that big vocal sound again… more so than in the last couple of years. We were just checking out other areas.

Are there any producers who can guarantee you a hit?

RC: No, not Mike Curb, not Richard Perry. Right now Barry Gibb is red-hot and everybody wants to be produced by Barry Gibb. But how long will that last?

Richard, you wrote a country song, "Top Of The World," that was a number one record on Top 40. Country radio didn't play your version, but went on a version by Lynn Anderson. That is understandable because country radio didn't look at you as country artists. Why all of a sudden have they accepted "Sweet, Sweet Smile?" That has to be a weird experience for you.

RC: It was really quite exciting.

KC: Since "Top Of The World" we always try and get maybe one or two country things on an album because we like them. But having one come out as a single and do that without really even thinking about it is really a welcome surprise.

Is that your song?

RC: No, that's Juice Newton and Otha Young who wrote it.

So you were not openly romancing the country stations?

RC: No, not really. We always put a couple of country-flavored things on each album. We just did that on "Sweet, Sweet Smile" because we liked it that way. I felt it also needed a fiddle and a banjo and it started to come on the country charts.

Why did country radio go on this record as dramatically as they did? Wasn't there a country cover version they could have played by an established country act?

KC: No. In fact, when we heard the tune it was on a cassette run-off from Juice's album and it was the only tune in the album that was hers and really appealed to us. So when we decided we wanted to do it, she held it off her album. So really, nobody knew about the tune and out it came.

Do you see yourself going more into country music as a result of your problems with Top 40?

KC: We wanted to cut something else country. We discussed it with the company. They said that would be terrific, but then all of a sudden everybody leaned on us for a country album, at which point Jerry Moss almost lost his hair. I mean, let's face it. Our first priority has to be to get a pop album. That is most important, but we definitely want to try country again. We love and enjoy doing country music.

Hollywood has discovered the recording industry. Do you see yourself getting involved in motion pictures?

KC: Yes, we're looking for a script. We have been for about a year. It's something I would really like to do. I love to act and sing. I'm not sure how or when it's going to come down, but I'd like to do a musical. Our all-time love is to do a college musical. It would be set in the 1970s. It would have to have modern technology plus a classic serial sci-fi approach.

Do you also want to act Richard?

RC: I wouldn't mind it, but not as much as Karen. My first love is the recording studio.

KC: I want to do some television acting, too. There have been a couple of scripts that were submitted, but I didn't have time to do them.

Do you think the record industry is qualified to make movies today?

KC: I think the record industry can handle anything that is put in front of them. They don't fall short of anything. This business is confronted with new things every hour.

Made In America

A&M Records Press Release (1981)

For Richard Carpenter, it was a day of triumph only a hardcore, lifelong musician could appreciate. After nearly a year of "listening, literally, to hundreds and hundreds of songs, my own writing, arranging, orchestrating; doing background vocals and piano, and mixing," the master tape of the new Carpenters album, their first in three years, had finally been put to bed and sent off to the manufacturing plants to become *Made In America*.

The title itself was revealing on a number of levels. It had turned up in one of those offhand, serendipitous flashes that seem to come from nowhere yet are right on the money. "We were playing around with any number of possible titles for the album," said Richard, "when Karen came into the studio one day wearing a running suit that read 'Made In America,' and I said, 'That's it!'"

Regarding *Made In America*, Richard says: "It's a very American sound – even more so, a California sound. We've been classified as a classic California sound. I have to agree with that." And in spite of recent shifts and trends in popular music, he feels that "things really aren't that different than they have been. There are a couple of things that have a little twist that I enjoy, like the Police, but nothing really that radically different."

And if *Made In America* is not "radically different" – refusing to pay homage to the weirder pop trends that come and go like summer lightning – it clearly documents the depth, growth and striving for perfection that characterizes all of the best of the Carpenters' work. Richard sums it up simply: "I select songs that hit me at the gut level and fit our style." The album includes two new songs by he and John Bettis: "Those Good Old Dreams," a tune Richard suggests has the flavor of "Top Of The World" and "Because We Are In Love," which they wrote expressly for Karen's wedding last year to Tom Burris.

The Carpenters' current hit single, "Touch Me When We're Dancing," was one of several tunes selected for *Made In America* penned by outside writers. Burt Bacharach contributed "Somebody's Been Lyin'," with lyrics by Carole Bayer Sager, and Richard believes "it's one of the best things

Bacharach has written in years." Also included is a new Roger Nichols/ Bill Lane song, "When You've Got What It Takes," that sounds like an instant classic.

The remainder of the tunes, with the exception of the old Marvelettes' hit, "Beechwood 4-5789," were written by various relatively new writers: "Strength Of A Woman." by Phyllis Brown and Juanita Curiel, and a lovely new country/pop ballad, "When It's Gone (It's Just Gone)," with words and music by Randy Handley.

"Karen and I think it's the best thing we've ever done," Richard says. "It's the combination of production, performance, engineering and material. It's just that you grow, you hear more things, you grow in your arranging, and Karen, of course, grows in her interpretation. You just grow…"

Part Four:
Rainy Days
And Mondays

Karen Carpenter Dies In Downey

By Pat McGreevy

Downey Herald American (1983)

Singer Karen Carpenter, who joined brother Richard for a string of musical hits in the 1970s, died suddenly of a heart attack Friday morning while visiting her parents at the Downey home she and her brother built for them. The sudden death of the popular musician, at 32 years of age, was a shock to her fans and friends, many of whom grew up with her in Downey.

Downey Police Department Detective Gary Morrow, who was present during the autopsy Friday, said the preliminary determination of cause of death was pulmonary edema, the medical term for the sudden stoppage of breathing and heartbeat. He said Carpenter had recently been treated for anorexia nervosa, an extreme weight loss condition where the person does not eat properly to force the loss of weight. The autopsy found her to be five-feet, four-inches tall and 108 pounds.

Although Carpenter had eaten regularly the week before her death, Morrow said an investigation is continuing as to the cause of her death, focusing both on the anorexia and the presence of prescription medicine found in her bloodstream. Her Downey physician, Dr. G.A. Monnet, had no comment on Carpenter's death.

Carpenter had arrived in Downey at the Newville Avenue house of her parents, Agnes and Harold Carpenter, on Thursday for a short overnight visit, according to her agent Paul Bloch. Ms. Carpenter awoke in the second floor bedroom of the large Downey house at approximately 8:10 a.m. Friday but collapsed approximately 30 minutes later on the floor in a closet of the bedroom where her parents found her minutes later, according to Downey Police and Fire Department officials.

The Downey Fire Department received the call from her parents at 8:51 a.m., and sent Engine Company No. 64 and a paramedics unit to the house near the San Gabriel River. Paramedics and an Adams Ambulance crew found Carpenter unconscious but with a slight pulse and began performing cardiopulmonary resuscitation (C.P.R.) before transporting her and her concerned mother, with full lights and siren, to the Downey Community Hospital emergency room.

A hospital spokesman said that when Carpenter arrived at the hospital at 9:23 a.m., she was in full cardiac arrest, not breathing and without a heartbeat. A medical team worked on her for 28 minutes but at 9:51 a.m. she was pronounced dead. Her body was turned over to the county coroner's office for an autopsy Friday and later released to Utter-McKinley Funeral Home in Downey. The family had not released the details of funeral arrangements as of Friday night.

Carpenter's sudden death was a complete shock to friends and business associates. "She was so young and healthy and had everything to look forward to," said Joan Jaffe, a spokeswoman for Carpenter's agent. Her agent said that Carpenter had been treated for anorexia last year and that in 1975, the Carpenters had to cancel a concert tour because Ms. Carpenter suffered from physical and emotional exhaustion for which she was hospitalized for several weeks.

Jaffe said Karen and Richard Carpenter were planning to go into the studio at A&M Records next month to begin recording a new album, which was to be followed by a tour of the United States this summer. "I was totally taken by surprise," said Carpenter's agent of 12 years, Paul Bloch. "She was young and healthy. She was squeaky clean as anybody who would do milk commercials would be."

Although her agent said she had not had a history of heart ailments, acquaintances said she had recently returned from New York where she had undergone treatment for anorexia. "She wanted to keep it quiet," said one acquaintance. Carpenter had also recovered from her divorce of Los Angeles businessman Thomas Burris, Jaffe said.

Those who saw her in Downey in recent months said she was in good spirits. In fact, last year Ms. Carpenter recorded a solo album with producer Phil Ramone in New York, which mysteriously was never released. Her agent would not say what the plans were for that album.

Like several other young musicians of the late '60s and early '70s, Karen and Richard Carpenter rose meteorically to success from their teenage years with the Downey High School Band to their big break in 1969 after Ms. Carpenter and her brother had gone on to Long Beach State to study music.

Since 1969, the Carpenters put their sweet, clean-cut sound on ten albums, eight of which were gold albums selling over 500,000 copies each. In 1970 the Carpenters had their biggest success, "Close To You."

Karen Carpenter played drums and sang for the duo while her brother sang and played the piano. Their albums continued to sell well into the mid-seventies. Jaffe said Karen and Richard Carpenter were confident that their new album would do well. "She was always positive and cheerful. She was looking forward to her new start," her agent said.

The sudden death of Ms. Carpenter from heart failure at age 32 stunned not only the musical industry and her many fans, but also the many friends and acquaintances she made during her Downey childhood. Whether it was her enthusiasm on the Downey High School Band, or her close relationship with her family, recollections of Carpenter's youth in Downey by friends painted the picture of a bright, happy woman with a gift for music.

When Harold and Agnes Carpenter moved to Downey from Connecticut with their children Richard and Karen in 1964, they settled in a cozy house near Rockwell International, according to friends. Karen was enrolled as a ninth grader at South Junior High School while her brother went to Downey High School, recalled Bruce Gifford, a long time music teacher at Downey High School who coached both Carpenters while they played in the school's band.

"He (Richard) originally wanted to play the trumpet but he was such a fine pianist that he stayed with that instrument," Gifford said. "When she came to Downey High School, Karen wanted to be in the band like her brother. She played the bells her first year in the band and then went on to play the drums," Gifford said. "Karen was the typical student, but she didn't smoke or drink," he recalled. "She didn't strike me as musically talented at first but then I've learned to give people time before judging their talent. And you know what happened to them."

Gifford said the striking thing about Karen Carpenter was the close family relationship she enjoyed. In the many times he had dinner with the Carpenters, he saw an unusual closeness in the family, which he says few kids enjoy.

Karen Carpenter graduated from Downey High School in 1967 and went on to Long Beach State where she and her brother put together the band with which they received their lucky break. Because the Carpenters' peak in popularity was nearly a decade ago, many of today's Downey High School students hadn't heard of her before her death. Those that had were stunned by her death at such a young age.

The Carpenters' success and the resulting wealth didn't keep Karen and Richard from their friends and family in Downey. In December of 1971, Karen and Richard Carpenter presented the City of Downey with a gold record for "Close To You," which in still on display in the trophy case at City Hall. The two musicians were grand marshals in the Downey Christmas Parade that year.

With the money they made from their first million-seller, the Carpenters bought two apartment buildings on Fifth Street, between Downey and Brookshire Avenues, which they named "Close To You" and "Only Just Begun." They also used a portion of their newfound wealth to build a magnificent house for their parents on Newville Avenue next to the San Gabriel River in Downey. The large house was equipped with state-of-the-art musical recording and listening equipment and a garage to contain Richard's automobiles.

Downey Optometrist Art Fry was shocked by Carpenter's death. He has known the Carpenter kids for 18 years and just fitted Karen Carpenter with glasses last month. "She was a real nice kid," Fry said. "They kept to themselves and never drank or smoked. They would always be home here for the holidays and every other important family occasion."

"I couldn't believe it. She was in here a week and a half ago looking as healthy as ever," said Jim Ayres, the owner of Foxy's Restaurant on Paramount Boulevard in Downey. "I talked to her then and she said she was fine," Ayres said. "She was in with her mother. They always came here for breakfast." Ayres described her as "bouncy and very energetic. She would talk to anybody. She was real friendly," he said. "Her death at such a young age really upsets me."

Hundreds Attend
Karen Carpenter Rites

Southeast News (1983)

Karen Carpenter, who sang with her brother as one of America's top pop music acts in the 1970s, was remembered Tuesday at her funeral in Downey as "one of God's most gifted and talented creations."

About 700 friends, family members and fans – among them some of the greatest names in the recording industry – packed the Downey United Methodist Church on Downey Avenue just blocks from the house where Ms. Carpenter once lived. Hundreds of other fans stood outside behind police barricades. Following the service, a small contingent of family members traveled by cortege to Forest Lawn Memorial Park in Cypress for a brief private ceremony before entombment.

Present at the 1:00 p.m. services for Ms. Carpenter were such singing and songwriting stars as Olivia Newton-John, Burt Bacharach, Dionne Warwick, John Bettis and John Davidson. Record industry executives like Jerry Weintraub, bandleader and A&M Records co-founder Herb Alpert, A&M President Gil Friesen and Mike Curb also were in attendance. Other friends of the Carpenters in attendance were ice skating star Dorothy Hamill and former Mouseketeer and Carpenters' drummer Cubby O'Brien.

Richard Carpenter, 36, accompanied his mother Agnes and father Harold into the church's main sanctuary, while adjacent rooms and a courtyard – all equipped with speakers broadcasting the service – were filled with approximately 500 fans who wanted to pay their last respects.

"What Karen loved she did resemble, until Karen herself became a song to the world – a beautiful song to the world," said the Reverend Charles Neal, Ms. Carpenter's childhood minister in New Haven, Connecticut, during his eulogy. "In the words of (songwriter) John Bettis, 'Too soon and too young our Karen is still, but her echo will linger forever.'"

"One of God's most gifted and talented creations is gone. The world weeps because Karen's story graced this world. She has captured the hearts of the world with friendship, love and joy. Karen stood for integrity, a quality of

175

life that is so refreshing. She has graced all of our lives with love and song and there is no place on Earth where Karen is not singing."

Neal recalled he first met Karen Carpenter when she and her brother were part of the Methodist youth ministry that welcomed him to his new church in New Haven, where she was born. He said Ms. Carpenter's childhood was "a balance of blue jeans, baseballs and ballet," and when the family got together in the basement of their New Haven home there would be "ping pong sets, hi-fi sets, baseballs and more records than I've ever seen in my life."

At one point Neal looked at her white metal casket, covered with red and white roses, and quoted the lyrics of one of the Carpenters' greatest hits, "Close To You" – "On the day that you were born the angels got together and decided to create a dream come true." The minister also recited the words to "We've Only Just Begun." "She graced this world with a new song," Neal said. "Suddenly in the midst of the rock era she brought a new song, a new sound of joy, happiness and meaning."

Reverend Michael Winstead, minister of the Downey United Methodist Church, also spoke at the service. He delivered the invocation and read several Bible passages, including Psalm 100 which begins "Make a joyful noise unto the Lord," and a section of Romans including the promise that "nothing shall be able to separate us from the love of God."

The choir from Cal State Long Beach, Ms. Carpenter's alma mater, sang "Adoramus Te" by Corsi and soloist Dennis Heath sang "Ave Maria" by Bach. Tuesday's service was preceded by an instrumental medley of Carpenters songs including, "Rainy Days And Mondays," "Close To You," and "We've Only Just Begun."

Pallbearers at the service included Herb Alpert, who signed a contract with the Carpenters at the beginning of their music career, and songwriter John Bettis, who wrote the lyrics for many of the Carpenters' songs. Other pallbearers included Steven Alpert, Werner Wolfen (Carpenter's attorney), Gary Sims, Eddie Sulzer (the duo's first manager), David Alley and Ed Leffler. Honorary pallbearers included Ms. Newton-John, Bacharach, former California Lieutenant Governor Curb, Hamill and O'Brien.

Many of the hundreds of mourners who attended the service or stood outside were fans in their 20s and 30s who remembered Ms. Carpenter from their youth. Many carried rose bouquets. "When I was growing up she kind of understood what I was going through in her songs," explained one fan, Mary Grouch. Another, Earl Storm, said he attended the funeral "just to thank her for the beauty she gave to my life."

176

A Lesson In Art Of Emotion: Karen Carpenter's Intimate Vocals Disarm A Critic

By Robert Hilburn

Los Angeles Times (1983)

I understood my sadness when Elvis Presley and John Lennon died. Along with Bob Dylan, they were my biggest pop heroes in the '50s and '60s. In their best moments, they not only lived up to the standards that I applied as a critic to pop acts, they defined them. I still listened regularly to their records and I had met them: Presley briefly backstage during one of his Las Vegas engagements and Lennon on several occasions.

But I was unsettled last week by my sadness when I learned about Karen Carpenter's death on February 4th. It wasn't just the flash of sympathy that invariably follows someone's death.

On a professional level, I try to resist the type of sentimentality that leads you to praise a lot of mediocre artists just because they've died. Such praise reduces all artists to a meaningless common denominator.

My sense of loss after Karen's death was genuine. The reason I was surprised by the reaction was that I wasn't, as a critic, someone you could even remotely list as a supporter of the Carpenters.

So why was I touched?

I dug out some Carpenters albums and listened to them again. In the process, I began reflecting on the differences between the demands made upon artists by a critic (who examines pop achievement) and regular listeners (who simply want to be entertained).

Critics want artists to challenge traditions so that we can gain insights or be inspired. It isn't enough merely to be handed already familiar emotions and techniques. That's generally why the Carpenters' records were downgraded by critics. Sweet and understated, the music usually lacked the boldness or social examination that critics prize. Except when reviewing their new releases, I rarely played their albums.

After Karen's death, however, I found myself thinking about her voice, even recalling the first time I heard it on the radio in a 1969 version of "Ticket To Ride." Unlike the Beatles' uptempo rendition, this one had the softer, plaintive quality of many a Mamas and Papas ballad.

The attraction for me was the intimacy and warmth of Karen's singing – a strange, but seductive blend of innocence and melancholia. But "Close To You," the record that launched the Carpenters' Top 10 reign later the same year, wasn't nearly as convincing. It had a timid, almost bloodless quality that was all too characteristic of the duo's recordings. After a while, I gave up on them.

But you really couldn't escape the Carpenters' sound because their records were all over the radio dial. Some tunes seemed catchy: the upbeat country tone of "Top Of The World" and the lazy disappointment of "Rainy Days And Mondays."

It wasn't until the *Passage* album in 1977, however, that I was really impressed by what Richard and Karen had done. Though it wasn't their biggest seller, the album contained some experimental touches that added refreshing character to their musical foundation.

On their version of "Don't Cry For Me, Argentina" from that album, there's a maturity to Karen's vocal that was far beyond anything in the early years. Even the song's lyrics have a chilling quality when considered in light of what we've learned about her in recent days.

I'm referring here to the move from a Southern California sheltered life to New York, where she battled for independence while struggling against post-marriage depression and anorexia nervosa, the dieting compulsion that caused her to drop from her normal 110-pound range to less than 85 pounds.

But that's not the song pointed out last weekend by John Bettis, who co-wrote many of the Carpenters' hits. When asked which of Karen's vocals was the most personal, he mentioned "I Need To Be In Love," a modest hit from 1976.

He said it was written at a time when the Carpenters were established as one of the biggest-selling pop groups ever, but that he and Richard and Karen all felt an emptiness. The words he wrote for her: "I know I ask for perfection of a quite imperfect world, and (I'm) fool enough to think that's what I'll find."

On these records, her voice conveys a heartwarming cry for understanding and love, a cry that struck a chord in millions of listeners who were unburdened by any sense of critical responsibility.

Though the moment didn't invalidate for me the need to seek out artists who challenge tradition and redirect our thinking, it did remind me that purity of emotion also is powerful.

Karen's voice may not have challenged pop tradition the way the critic in me would have preferred, but the loveliness of her best vocals did enrich us. The loss is real. It's also instructive: The heart of pop music is emotion and you can never measure emotion by critical standards alone.

Robert Hilburn has been a pop music critic for The Los Angeles Times *since 1970.*

Little Drummer Girl: Memories Of Karen

By Robyn Flans
Modern Drummer (1983)

On February 4th, Karen Carpenter died of cardiac arrest. Reports have linked her weak heart to a disease from which she suffered, but supposedly had overcome: anorexia nervosa, the compulsion to be thin.

Like many, I only knew Karen through her music and her smooth, stirring vocals on such songs as "Close To You," "For All We Know," "Rainy Days And Mondays," and "Goodbye To Love." I can't recall the number of brides and grooms I saw walk down the aisle to "We've Only Just Begun," and I recall how the depth of her emotion on "Superstar" touched my adolescent heart.

I want to express my gratitude to those I contacted who knew Karen and worked with her and were willing to answer questions and share memories in a time of personal loss. Bassist Joe Osborn recorded Richard and Karen Carpenter in his garage studio while they were still in high school. "Karen always had a terrific style," he recalls. Osborn wanted to help them and constantly told his fellow session musician, the legendary drummer Hal Blaine, about these two special kids – Richard on organ and Karen on drums and vocals.

"I met Karen during the Jimmy Webb session of 'MacArthur Park,' I believe," Hal remembers. "Joe invited them over to the studio because he had always told me about them and said we should do something with them. He wanted me to produce them. We talked and they were very nice, but I said to Joe, 'How in the heck are we going to go into the studio and produce them when we're doing four, five and six sessions a day?'"

But both Osborn and Blaine ended up playing on the Carpenters' records when A&M signed them, with producer Jack Daugherty at the helm. Their first album, *Offering*, made some noise and paved the way for their second album, *Close To You*. Enter Hal Blaine.

"When they decided to go with professional musicians, they had talked to Karen about my playing drums, and as far as she was concerned, it was fine because they wanted a hit. Her mother was upset at first and said, 'I've watched drummers on TV for years and Karen is as good as any of them.' She didn't understand that there were different techniques involved, but eventually she understood.

"I've always said Karen was a good drummer to begin with. Often times, guys think that a girl drummer isn't right, no matter what. But I knew she could play right away when she'd sit down at my drums on sessions. She played a lot of the album cuts as well, and we had Howie Oliver make her up a set of my monster drums. But about the third or fourth hit, I remember I said to her, 'When are you going to get off the drums? You sing too good and you should be fronting the band.'"

Enter Cubby O'Brien. Cubby was asked to join the road band in 1973 and also recorded some of the album tracks, remaining with them even after they stopped touring around 1979.

"Karen was very knowledgeable about the drums and was a very good drummer, there's no doubt about that. Some of the things we did together were not easy. Richard wanted it exactly the way it was on record. When I first joined the group, Karen was still playing in the show. We worked out all the drum breaks from the records and I played exactly what she did. The idea of getting me was to actually get her off the drums, and in order to do that, they needed a strong drummer. Richard had grown up with her playing and thought a lot of it, so it was hard for somebody else to take over that chair.

"But at one time, playing was a very big issue in her life. I remember one time Karen and I went to see Buddy Rich and Louie Bellson's band. I know Buddy fairly well, so before the show, I took Karen to meet him backstage. He was getting ready when I introduced her, 'Buddy, this is Karen Carpenter.' And he said, 'Karen Carpenter! You're one of my favorite drummers, you know that?' When we got back to our seats, Karen turned to me and said, 'Was he putting me on?'

"Karen was a very special person. She was always a very happy, very up person, even when things were bad. Her death shocked me and really saddened me. I spoke to her just four or five days before she died and she was feeling good and much stronger than she had felt. She wasn't getting as tired as she had in the past, and all the way around, things were straightening out. She and Richard were making plans to perform and thinking of going over to Japan and playing out of the country first."

In 1969, a woman drummer was unheard of. Today, in 1983, it is still unusual. It does, in fact, take a lot of courage for a woman to pursue that instrument when the stereotypes are so difficult to penetrate. "Karen hated for somebody to say, 'You're really good – for a woman,'" Cubby said. "Nobody better have said that!"

Karen Goes On –
Thirty Minutes With
Richard Carpenter

By Pat McGreevy
Southeast News (1983)

As Richard Carpenter climbed onto an England-bound plane recently for a stint to promote the Carpenters' latest and last album, it suddenly struck him – this was the first time his sister Karen was not going along on a promotional or concert tour.

"That's when it really struck me," the singer said during an interview at his Downey home late last week. "It was tough… it really was. Once I had to go to England and Japan alone for press conferences in 1975 when Karen got ill, and we had to cancel or postpone two major tours. But that was different. This was actually going out with a new album.

"We've worked together and we've always been close for the past 17 or 18 years, so it was rough. Karen and I were always the best of friends, as well as family."

The Carpenters' career reached its pinnacle in 1970 with the international hit "Close To You." "Neither of us needed any prodding," Carpenter said. "We loved performing. You basically had two very happy people anyway, and then to get a worldwide number one… I'd have to say that was the most exciting period of our lives – especially to have that at age 20 and 23."

Immediately after the interview, Carpenter had dinner with his parents, Harold and Agnes Carpenter, and then climbed aboard a plane for a promotional tour of Japan. "It's Japan and then Australia, then home for a day and off to New York," Richard said. On the den wall above where he sat was a large framed assemblage of the group's gold records.

Carpenter was at home for only five days last week between promotional tours. One of those days was proclaimed "Carpenters Day" by the Los Angeles City Council. That day, Carpenter accepted a star dedicated to him and his sister on Hollywood Boulevard's Walk of Fame. "It was really special, although it was also sad with Karen not there," he said.

185

Richard's globe-hopping is to promote the final Carpenters album, *Voice Of The Heart*, soon to be released in the United States. In England, the album debuted two weeks ago at number 11 on that country's album chart.

Karen completed recording several of the vocal tracks on the album just before her death. Her brother went back to the studio after his sister's death and arranged, produced and recorded the instrumental and backup vocal tracks. Richard wrote three of the songs on the new album and arranged nine of them. "It would have been a crime to let it sit on a shelf," he said. "Karen had some wonderful vocals. A lot of people were looking forward to the new album."

The pop performer said that while "The Carpenters" are now a fond memory, he has no intention of retiring. He plans to continue playing solo concerts with orchestras, performing pop and light classical music and writing songs as well as arranging and producing records for himself and other artists. He even plans to explore the possibility of performing on television specials and composing musical scores for films.

"Mainstream pop" is how Richard describes the sound of Karen's drums and vocals and his piano, vocal and string arrangements. "It was never earthshakingly new," he said. " It did have a different sound, but it was still in an established genre. It's not progressive. It's traditional pop. I like that. I'm proud of that kind of music. It's a lasting art form. Look at Air Supply. They really sound Carpenteresque."

Richard said the music of the Carpenters strikes a familiar chord in the hearts of people worldwide. "It's the ballads and love songs that have been sung over the ages," he said. Even in countries like Japan, audiences enjoyed the Carpenters' concerts and albums, he said. "There's something in the music that ties it together. Like they say, music is the universal language."

When success came, however, Richard kept his ties to his family and friends and stayed in Downey, although he moved into a larger home. He still collects automobiles, a hobby he has enjoyed for years. "I'm a homebody, and I'm very comfortable in this town," he said. "It's peaceful here. It's nice to come out of it all into a quiet community. So when things broke loose I didn't want to move to Beverly Hills. We're a close family, and it's nice to be near my parents."

"I was stunned," Richard said, recalling his sister's untimely death. "A 32-year-old woman falling over with heart failure – especially since she had never smoked, drank or used drugs. It was baffling." He said he and his parents had worried over his sister's long struggle with anorexia nervosa, an illness she was struggling over even when the pair's career was skyrocketing.

186

"It's insidious and perplexing," Richard said of the illness. "The researchers are trying, and they're learning new things." Toward that end, the family set up the Karen Carpenter Memorial Foundation, which has been receiving contributions toward musical scholarships at Long Beach State and for research into the cause of anorexia nervosa. Richard said the family received several letters from the families of anorexic persons after Ms. Carpenter's death. "Her death drew world attention to the disorder," he said.

Carpenter said the nature of art has helped him live with his sister's death. "Karen's death was a tragedy. But the least I can say is that we had been fortunate to have the opportunity to record. As a result of that, it's there – it's there forever. That's terrific. In one way, Karen goes on."

She'd Only Just Begun: Fine CBS Movie Tells Sad Story Of Karen Carpenter

By Ron Miller

San Jose Mercury News **(1989)**

The death of singer Karen Carpenter in 1983 from complications of an eating disorder remains one of the saddest and most bewildering episodes in pop music history. Carpenter had one of the richest, most beautiful voices of her time, and today, nearly six years after her death, she's still heard on the nation's easy-listening stations, where her many hits are evergreen standards.

It's hard to associate that serene sound with the troubled soul behind it. On February 4th, 1983 she was so weak and physically ruined that her heart simply stopped beating. Why would a rich, good-looking and phenomenally successful 32-year-old starve herself in a manic quest for thinness? What went wrong?

That's the question posed by tonight's CBS movie of the week, *The Karen Carpenter Story*, a moving film biography of Carpenter that comes up with a number of possible explanations, most of them credible, all of them tragic.

Though the film was produced by Carpenter's brother, Richard, her creative partner in their immensely popular recording duo, the Carpenters, it seems to pull few punches.

It deals with Richard's addiction to Quaaludes as well as Karen's illness, anorexia nervosa, a psychologically motivated form of self-starvation peculiar to young women. It's also hard on their parents, Agnes and Harold Carpenter, who dominated their lives well into adulthood.

In many ways, the teleplay by Barry Morrow suggests that neither Richard nor Karen were very mature when their music thrust them into the spotlight, leaving them ill-prepared to cope with the stresses of superstardom and the strain of long road tours.

It shows us a childishly insecure Karen, failing at marriage while abusing herself with severe dieting, diuretics, laxatives and endless exercise in what may have been a subconscious attempt to prove herself the master of at least one thing in an overly controlled life – her own body. Along the way it also hints that the older brother and younger sister were so psychologically dependent on one another that they were unable to relate normally to others.

If there's an arch-villain of the story, it's probably Agnes Carpenter (Louise Fletcher), an imposing woman who found it almost impossible to show her love to her troubled daughter, even after her illness had been diagnosed and the threat to her life was clear.

The mother is also seen giving her own prescription drugs to Richard to help him sleep, and later refusing to accept her son's addiction to the drugs, even after Karen tells her about it.

Mrs. Carpenter dominates her placid husband, Harold (Peter Michael Goetz), and shows the force of her personality in an early scene in which a recording contract is offered to Karen but not to her older brother. She comes close to killing the deal outright but ends up making sure Karen knows she's only half of a team that she won't allow to be separated.

The film shows Richard as protective but not above jealousy. Though it's clear that Richard's keen musical sense developed the trademark sound of the Carpenters, it's also clear Karen was the star. Yet when she hints at going out as a solo act while he's hospitalized, Richard is stunned and hurt. He bullies her out of it, convincing her that she, too, needs rest. She does, but his motives may not be completely unselfish in talking her into it.

After a while, it becomes clear that Karen carried an enormous psychological burden. An apparently sweet, naive and good-natured young woman is transformed into a self-destructive neurotic by her failure to reconcile her inability to find love while being loved by millions.

The film is buttressed by two superb performances in the leading roles. Cynthia Gibb, a graduate of TV's "Fame" and one of the most capable young actresses in Hollywood, makes the tortured Karen into a personal triumph. Gibb is a terrific musical performer herself, but mostly lip-syncs Karen's original recordings in a series of nicely staged musical sequences. Richard is played engagingly by newcomer Mitchell Anderson.

The movie picks up Carpenter's story in 1963 when the family moved from Connecticut to Downey, in Southern California, partly to be near the entertainment industry, where they hoped that the talented Richard could "become a superstar."

At 13, Karen makes her debut singing "End Of The World." Doubling on drums, the Richard Carpenter Trio wins a Hollywood "battle of the bands." They get a studio audition, but the label is really interested only in the magnetic vocals by young Karen.

The story carries them through their meteoric rise on the pop charts after a boost from bandleader Herb Alpert, who gave them Burt Bacharach's "Close To You" to record, their first mega-hit.

Later, the film recounts the moment when Richard saw a Crocker Bank commercial on TV at 2:00 a.m. and was inspired to adapt the tune for the Carpenters. It became "We've Only Just Begun," another million-seller.

Also depicted is Karen's reluctance to get up and stand in front of the band to sing. Richard and their managers had to conspire to pry her away from her drums and get her out front where she belonged.

Her shyness obviously was a part of Karen's problem. After reading a review in *Billboard* that refers to her as Richard's "chubby sister," she launches herself on an obsessive weight-loss program.

Through the film, director Joseph Sargent neatly uses the Carpenters' lyrics to accentuate the psychological climate of Karen's life. In one inspired sequence, Sargent offers a montage showing the breakdown of Karen's marriage while she sings "This Masquerade" on the soundtrack with its doubly meaningful lyrics ("We tried to talk it over, but the words got in the way...").

Though the film strives to avoid pessimism and remain entertaining, it still carries an emotional wallop, particularly in the closing sequence when the family shares a holiday dinner and Karen's mother tries to make up for lost time with her troubled daughter.

The Karen Carpenter Story is an above-average TV drama about a seemingly normal person who somehow went off the tracks on her way to the top of the world. It reminds us how little we really know about the dark side of the gifted people we admire so much.

Karen Was Wasting Away... I Had A Drug Problem...And We Couldn't Help Each Other

By **Richard Carpenter**

TV Guide **(1988)**

I called her K.C., and she called me R.C. It seems as if we did everything together. We loved cars and went bowling and listened to Spike Jones, Nat King Cole and Elvis, among many others. More than brother and sister, we were best friends. Karen and I still lived with our parents when we recorded "Close To You," "We've Only Just Begun" and quite a few of the subsequent hits. In 1974, we bought a house together and it seemed we couldn't miss. Yet it wasn't too long after we hit the peak of success that we were both careening down separate paths of destruction – me on sleeping pills and Karen starving herself. Our career was over long before I thought it would end.

Karen's death is still a mystery to me. If she had died in a more tangible way – if she had been hit by a car – it would have been equally tragic but something I could comprehend. The eating disorder that killed her, anorexia nervosa, was little understood then and only a little more now.

What would possess a woman like her to starve herself? Some people blame it on career pressures or a need to take more control over her life. I don't think so. I think she would have suffered from the same problem even if she had been a homemaker. She was not always a slave to her self-image. Sure, she had been concerned about her weight since she was a teenager and had dieted to lose her childhood chubbiness. Karen lost 25 pounds on a water diet when she was 17. Her weight remained stable, and she continued to eat sensibly.

By 1975, it was clear something was seriously wrong with her. We canceled part of our world tour that year because Karen was frail and tiring easily. She spent weeks in bed while my parents and I tried to coax her into eating. That was when we first learned about anorexia. Much has been written about the disorder since Karen's death. But back then, we had little to go on.

It wasn't much later that I realized I also was ruining my life through behavior I couldn't control. I had become addicted to Quaaludes, which I had begun taking to help me sleep after our first European tour. I continued taking the pills at night for several years without any problems, but my body was building up a tolerance to them and I found myself taking more than the prescribed dosage to achieve the desired effect. As a result, the drug would take longer to wear off the following day. My speech would become slurred and my hands would start trembling. I couldn't write anymore and had trouble performing. One side of me was saying, "You fool. You're killing yourself, you can't function, and you're letting your sister and parents down." But the other side convinced me I couldn't get by without those pills.

While I was trying to prevent Karen from withering away, she was trying to help me kick my drug dependency. I tried a couple of detox programs, but even if you get the stuff out of your system, it's hard to lick the problem. By 1978, I was in trouble, no two ways about it. We were playing at the MGM Grand in Las Vegas and I had reached the point where I couldn't stop slurring until about 5 p.m., and then all I could think about was going back to bed. Each night, all I wanted to do was get off that stage. We cancelled halfway through the engagement, sent all the musicians home and left the room dark. I made up some excuse – like I was exhausted or something – and didn't think twice about it. This is totally unlike me, before and since.

At Christmas that year, Karen and I were going to do a benefit concert for the Carpenters Choral Scholarship Fund at our alma mater, California State University at Long Beach. We were set to play with the school's symphony and choir. As the day of the show drew closer, I started removing songs from the program because I couldn't perform them. My hands were shaking too much. I told Karen I was dropping "It's Christmas Time" because I didn't think it would go over well. And I told her I was dropping "The Nutcracker" because I didn't think the university orchestra could cut it. I pared that damn program down to almost nothing because I couldn't play most of it.

Poor Karen. She was buying all of this, even though she knew I had a problem. I always had excuses for everything. You get pretty devious – the same way anorexics do. But it finally got so bad that I couldn't get out of bed and I had to say, "Karen, I've got a problem here." So I checked into the chemical dependency unit at the Menninger Clinic in Topeka, Kansas. That was in early 1979.

It wasn't until her brief marriage ended in 1981 that Karen decided she needed help. She moved to New York to start daily sessions with a therapist who specialized in anorexia. But the treatment didn't take. When she came home around Thanksgiving, 1982, she was heavier. But it wasn't the sign of a cure – she had been fed intravenously. Even with the added weight, she always appeared fatigued.

I remember so clearly the morning she died. She had called me the day before from her condominium. She was going to buy a new VCR and wanted to know what I recommended. Then we talked for a while. I guess she decided later to drive down and spend the night at our folks' house. My mother called me the next morning and, of course, she was hysterical. She had found Karen unconscious on the closet floor in the bedroom. I remember driving over to the house, hoping against hope that it was just a collapse. I even thought that maybe it would be something serious enough to move her to seek treatment again. I got there just as they were bringing her out of the house on a gurney.

Making a movie about all this has been an emotional roller coaster. I've had to stir up a lot of memories – joyous ones as well as painful. But I realized soon after Karen's death that if I didn't make the movie, someone else would, and I wanted to make sure it was done as accurately as possible. I also gave long and hard thought to whether Karen would have wanted her story told. I think she would have. She was an honest person and not afraid to show her down side. She might also have seen this as a way to help others suffering from anorexia. And besides, it was in her makeup. I guess this goes for both of us.

Carpenters Telepic
Boosts Record Sales

Variety (1989)

One month after *The Karen Carpenter Story* aired on CBS to high ratings, the Carpenters' catalog of hit albums is still selling at roughly two times its normal rate, after surging some 400% in the two weeks immediately following the January 1st telecast.

"It's almost like she died all over again," said Kathy Dosdall, a national buyer for the 630-store Musicland/Sam Goody chain. "We rarely see sales like this just from a TV show."

Dosdall said the operation was not prepared for the overwhelming response from the movie, which told of Karen Carpenter's losing battle with anorexia nervosa. "We ran out pretty quickly, so there's no telling how much we would have sold had we had the stuff on hand."

In some cities, the sales surge is being sustained by another film treatment of Karen Carpenter's life, *Superstar*. Director Todd Haynes' underground documentary, which uses Barbie and Ken dolls to portray Karen and her brother Richard, is playing to sold-out crowds at arthouses in San Francisco and Washington, D.C.

David Steffen, Senior V.P. of Sales and Distribution at A&M, the Carpenters' label and scene of some of the TV film's action, is hoping CBS reruns the show soon. "Sales on the entire catalog have more than doubled since it was broadcast," he said, though he would not reveal just how many units have moved as a result of the TV pic.

Unfortunately for Steffen and the rest of the folks at A&M, the popularity of the program did little to boost sales of Richard Carpenter's recent solo album for the label, *Time*.

Part Five:
A Song
For You

Yesterday, Once More

By Stephen Whitty
San Jose Mercury News **(1990)**

Sonic Youth recorded a tribute, "Tunic (Song For Karen)." A new greatest-hits package, *Only Yesterday*, went to number one in Britain. And there's a definitive, four-CD set due next year from A&M Records. Seven years after her death, nearly two decades after her greatest success, Karen Carpenter is a pop star.

Why the sudden interest? Well, there was that three-Kleenex TV-bio last year. "When you die so young," one record exec told *Entertainment Weekly*, "there is a sympathy factor." But the Carpenter cult is stronger than that. Maybe it's just an overdue appreciation of a singer who, despite some terrible material, always had a pure pop voice. Or maybe it's simply a twinge of '70s nostalgia – for baby boomers in their twenties, "Close To You" was part of their AM-radio childhoods. But the Carpenters are back.

And it's only just begun. Again.

Loyal Brother Brings Legacy Into The '90s

By Janet Wiscombe

Long Beach Press-Telegram (1994)

Wearing a relentlessly colorful Hawaiian shirt splashed with red hibiscus, white cotton pants with white socks and boat shoes, Richard Carpenter's cheerful Beach Boy image is oddly unsettling.

The Dutch-boy haircut is shorter now, and he's lost 20 pounds, but the eyes are still doleful, the posture a little stiff. Hard as he tries to be affable and accommodating, it's clear the pianist/composer would rather be anywhere else.

He's come to the Richard and Karen Carpenter Performing Arts Center on the California State University Long Beach campus today to talk about the Carpenters phenomenon and to reflect on his own life. Introspection does not come easy.

Saturday night he will be on stage with such friends as Herb Alpert, Marilyn McCoo and Rita Coolidge to perform at the center's gala premier. Last year he gave the university more than $1 million to help maintain the 1,162-seat multiuse theater. The building is far more than a handsome gift to his alma mater. It symbolizes a stunning new era propelling the squeaky-clean Carpenters into the unlikely world of alternative rock.

"The worldwide focus is now on our music rather than on Karen's personal problems," he says, referring to his sister's death after an eight-year battle with anorexia nervosa. "It's very nice for a change. Now people are talking about the music."

Since Karen's death at age 32 in 1983, he has spent much of his time at his palatial, 7,500-square-foot home/studio in Downey making albums and preparing compilations of Carpenters songs for release throughout the world. Even if he wanted to do something else, the public has almost demanded he remain loyal Brother Carpenter.

Affection for the brother-sister duo has never dimmed, particularly in the United Kingdom and Japan. With the publication of a biography earlier this year and the release this month of an all-star tribute album, the Carpenters once again have risen to rarefied heights. What's weird for all of those who remember them as bubbly all-American suburban kids is that the new album features 14 alternative-rock groups singing their versions of Carpenter oldies like "(They Long To Be) Close To You" and "Top Of The World." And the album is not campy or sarcastic. It is a respectful tribute to the Carpenters by rock acts – from Sonic Youth to the Cranberries – who genuinely love their subtle sound.

Carpenter, now a 47-year-old father of four, is clearly pleased. "I'm the Perry Como of my generation," he offers with a sweetly fragile smile.

Although the media had a field day psychoanalyzing the Carpenter family, using the name as a metaphor for the darker side of the American Dream, the Richard Carpenter Story has never been told. By his own description, he is a somewhat reclusive, nocturnal man with the metabolism of a hummingbird. He says he prefers being at home to traveling, and would rather play "It's A Small World" at his daughter's preschool than be on stage.

"I've always been a homebody," he says. "I've lived in Downey for 31 years. It has a small town feeling. I'm furniture here. I like to do ordinary stuff. I go to the grocery store. I go to PTA meetings." At the height of their career in the '70s, the Carpenters were releasing albums by the dozen, holding news conferences in Toyko, singing at the White House, banking millions.

It was only after Karen's death that Richard married his wife, Mary, and began a family. He is the very proud father of three young girls and a 2-month-old son. If asked what he does for a living, Carpenter jokingly says his kids would say he is a housekeeper or that he works on cars. And they would be right. "I usually have a sponge in my hand," he says. "I'm very fastidious, and we have a lot of glass coffee tables."

When not sequestered in the music room or tinkering in the warehouse he owns to store his fleet of classic cars, he usually can be found organizing, painstakingly organizing everything in sight. "I'm a bit persnickety," says the musician, known for his obsessive attention to detail. "I am the tender of the family photographs and history. I keep track of all the dates and the family books. All the music is ordered, labeled and put in alphabetical order."

In the new biography of the Carpenters, author Ray Coleman writes about how shocked and angered Richard was years ago when he was introduced as "Richard Carpenter, piano player with the Carpenters." Over the years there have been those who've identified Karen as the standout, Richard the backup. Nothing could be further from the truth, a close friend comments in the book. "As much as she was the voice, he was the genius."

With characteristic humility, Carpenter makes this observation: "Karen has a timeless voice. The combination of our voices was quite appealing. Karen's death was and is a tragedy," he adds. "There's really only so much that can be said. I miss her. I think about her every day. I have posters of her in the music room. She loved kids. She would have loved our kids."

He gazes at the dazzling windows at the entrance to the Richard and Karen Carpenter Performing Arts Center. "To be here in this building, to hear all of the new songs coming out… she would have loved it."

At the time he and Karen were students at Cal State in the '60s, they were far more interested in recording music than in reading books. He says he's just a few units shy of graduation. "One of these days I'd like to get my degree," he says. "And once the gala is wrapped up, I'm going to start writing music again. What's important to me is raising my family and writing music."

Editor's Note: On May 26, 2000, Richard Carpenter was presented with an honorary doctorate from the College of the Arts at California State University Long Beach. The Richard and Karen Carpenter Performing Arts Center is now home to the Carpenters Exhibit, a museum-quality display, showcasing Richard's Wurlitzer 140-B electronic piano, Karen's 1965 Ludwig Super Classic drum set and a sample of the many awards received by the Carpenters over the years.

That Whitebread Image Came With A Dark Side

By David Konjoyan
Orange County Register (1994)

Editor's Note: David Konjoyan was co-Executive Producer of the 1994 tribute album If I Were A Carpenter.

Not long ago, during an interview with Babes In Toyland drummer Lori Barbero, I compared her aggressive jackhammer musical technique to the soothing drum and vocal style of Karen Carpenter. It was a remark I was sure would goad her into some politically incorrect comments that would make good copy. To my surprise, she instead offered this glowing tribute: "Karen's one of my female musician idols," she told me without a trace of irony. "I know the words to tons of Carpenters songs."

It wasn't the first time remarks of adoration for the Carpenters were uttered by an unlikely source. In fact, over the last few years several artists have paid their own unique respects to the '70s pop hitmakers.

While it's easy to dismiss all of this as just more quirky campiness where the mediocrities of the past are celebrated as masterpieces of the present - "Here's a story of a man named Brady" and all that - there seems to be more to it than that.

On the recent soundtrack to *Even Cowgirls Get The Blues*, k.d. lang, a vocal Carpenters fan, sang the smoothly melodic "Hush Sweet Lover." She told MTV newscaster Kurt Loder it was a deliberate nod to the duo (an idea that Loder's dismissive facial expression made clear he didn't appreciate).

And Sonic Youth checked in with "Tunic (Song For Karen)" from their 1990 album *Goo*, an oddly touching elegy. Add to this comments of appreciation from Pretender Chrissie Hynde, Axl Rose, and members of the Dutch alternative band Bettie Serveert among others and *If I Were A Carpenter* was a record waiting to be made.

Critics have long pointedly insisted that only white, middle class, suburban kids (if any kids at all) could appreciate the Carpenters' homogenized pop. Though I disagree with such a simple assessment, they may have a point.

Given Karen's tragic life - which ended in 1983 at age 32 after her struggle with anorexia nervosa and the larger picture of low self-esteem and lack of control it reflects - the singer may in fact have been a symbol that all was not perfect in those Rockwell paintings of middle America.

Like David Lynch's "Twin Peaks," her story suggests that relative economic privilege does not equal total happiness. A number of the bands on *If I Were A Carpenter* probably grew up white suburban kids. It's not surprising they could relate to Karen's troubling story.

But above all else, there was the voice. Warm, intimate, inviting and pure but burnished with just a hint of sadness. Karen's voice contained a longing, melancholy quality, a richness and depth of emotion that rose defiantly, if somberly, from the surrounding easy-going pop.

It wasn't the earthier blues of the city but a true suburban blues that said life under the placid surface bubbled with its own sources of anguish and pain, and she spoke for a lot of us. Her singing has proven timeless and classic, and perhaps that, more than any other reason, explains the lasting power of the Carpenters' music.

Most of those who might be considered the Carpenters' contemporaries have quietly become golden oldies (Bread, Anne Murray, the Captain & Tennille) or are revived solely for their kitsch value (the Osmonds). Meanwhile, the Carpenters continue to sell millions of records worldwide every year.

Time has proven that the Carpenters stood on their own in what they did, and for that alone, they've earned respect. As Sonic Youth's Thurston Moore has said, "Even when you were a punk rocker you thought the Carpenters were cool."

Interpretations and Vindication: The *HITS* Interview With Richard Carpenter

By David Konjoyan
HITS (1994)

Who would have thought that when highly regarded producer Matt Wallace (Faith No More, The Replacements, John Hiatt) and I conceived *If I Were A Carpenter* (A&M), our alterna-spin on the Carpenters, it would strike more than just the two of us as a fun, inspired idea for an intriguing record. We were simply fans, and knew the artists who took part were as well. The story going around that has Matt and I meeting in high school singing Carpenter songs in the boys locker room has some basis in fact (though we categorically deny the nagging rumors we had Richard Nixon photos hanging in our lockers – Elvis Presley was as conservative as we got.) Since then, our musical tastes have expanded from the Carps to the Clash to Kurt Cobain and this seemed like a great chance to marry them all in an unlikely and surprising package that was inspired by pro-Carpenter comments in the music press from artists like Sonic Youth and Babes In Toyland. A&M responded to it as a hip way to celebrate the Carpenters' 25th Anniversary, and *If I Were A Carpenter* was born.

By the time we were done, cool artists, ranging from Sonic Youth, Redd Kross and Bettie Serveert to Grant Lee Buffalo, Shonen Knife and American Music Club, had joined the festivities. Of course, none of us knew as we embarked on the project what the Man himself – Richard Carpenter – would think. Would he like this quirky appreciation, or would he simply ignore or even disown it? We were gratified to discover that Richard enjoyed the record nearly track for track and truly appreciated its spirit and intent. He's been a gracious participant at a time when a quiet home life and a new baby are his biggest priorities, and he even granted this interview to *HITS*...

What was your initial reaction when the idea for If I Were A Carpenter *was explained to you?*

I didn't have any trouble with it. I have to be honest, I didn't think it was going to happen. As you know, there were two proposals – one for a so-called "mainstream" record and one for an alternative. And of course, just about everyone thought the one that was gonna fly would be the mainstream one.

Were you nervous at all about how the record might sound or what the intentions were?

After the initial meeting, I didn't think about it at all. Then a couple of months went by and I got a phone call from Diana [Baron], and then from David [Anderle], saying this thing had really been coming along. Then a couple of articles came out saying this was being done so they could make fun [of us], "tongue firmly planted in cheek," and so forth. Diana wanted me to talk to a few people and I said, "Look, if this whole thing's a send-up, I don't want to be involved." But she assured me, "Don't believe everything you read." Then I heard a couple of rough mixes and they struck me as honest. Then I got a call from [VP A&R] Larry Hamby about guesting on Matthew Sweet's track.

Since the Carpenters always took flack from critics, is it a vindication to have artists who are sort of the "pillars of cool" today pay tribute to you?

I don't know that I feel vindicated. On the whole, I don't have much to complain about. I think what this might do is at least show to some people that our music has a little more appeal to varying tastes than might have been thought.

One of the things that struck Matt and I as the tapes came in is that the bands managed to stay true to themselves without straying too far from your arrangements.

They all stayed true to themselves from what I could figure, but some of them actually did follow my road map on the tunes: [Grant Lee Buffalo's] "We've Only Just Begun," of course, and [Sonic Youth's] "Superstar," in its own way. [4 Non Blondes'] "Bless The Beasts" was quite a bit different from my arrangement. And I suppose I was expecting to hear more of that, but all of it seems from the heart.

I heard you might like Dishwalla's "It's Going Take Some Time" better than your own.

I do enjoy their interpretation every bit as much as ours, if not more. I really think they not only took a fresh and inspired approach to it, they sound like a bunch of talented people to me.

And Sonic Youth.

Again, it pretty much follows the original. But of course the vocal interpretation is quite different, but in its way, it works. It's a haunting song and lyric and Thurston's [Moore] half-sung, half-whispered vocal actually works very well. On some of the songs, I do hear some Beatles influence, particularly the "White Album." If anyone was listening to the radio at all growing up – and these bands certainly did – you were going to hear the Beatles and the Carpenters. Consciously or not, this stuff is assimilated.

These artists were fans already, but I sensed they came out of the studio with a new respect for the music and especially Karen's voice.

Whether one likes it or not, Karen and I performed this stuff well, and a lot of times that makes things seem easy. Some Carpenters songs sound simple. Well, they're not. Even a song like "Top Of The World" is not simple. Of course, Karen sang effortlessly. But once these artists started taking the songs apart, I can see how their appreciation might have grown.

When you think of bands influenced by the Carpenters, Babes In Toyland and Sonic Youth don't come immediately to mind. What's your take on how you might have influenced these artists?

It could be they just heard the songs on the radio and liked 'em. If you look back at the early '70s, you had Led Zeppelin and the Carpenters and the audience said, "I like both." That's something that tends to be forgotten today.

A lot of these artists seemed to relate to what they see as the "dark side" of the Carpenters – the sadder songs, the melancholy in Karen's voice.

The songs were selected first on the melody. If that got me, then I'd listen to the lyric. Karen's voice did have a built-in melancholia to it. It had a warmth, an intimacy, but also a sense of longing that really went beyond her years. You listen to Karen sing "Superstar" or "Rainy Days And Mondays" when she was maybe 21 – she just sounds much older than that.

211

How did you like working with Matthew Sweet?

Oh, very much. Immediately simpatico. Very nice fellow. Talented, down-to-earth, easy to talk with. Of course, we have a common interest in automobiles.

Matthew made a great comment regarding the atmosphere in the studio that day. He said it was like one of the Beatles came in.

Oh my. I can't imagine anyone feeling that way about me. I think most of us tend to think of ourselves as pretty average people. But I've met fans who actually shake in your presence and I think, "My God, it's just us. I mean, please settle down!" When Paul McCartney asked us to come by the studio in Manchester, we were world-famous and yet I took along my *Band On The Run* album to have him sign.

The idea for this record came from reading appreciative comments by k.d. lang, Chrissie Hynde and others in the press. Were you aware of this new generation of fans?

Oh yeah. Through the years people would mention to me that they read an article, maybe k.d. lang – of course, I'm a big fan of k.d., and it doesn't surprise me she'd be a fan of Karen's – and Gloria Estefan, Michael Jackson, Chrissie Hynde.

What would Karen have thought of *If I Were A Carpenter*?

She'd like it for the same reasons I like it – that the people involved thought enough of our music or her talent to take time out of their schedules to contribute, and that there continues to be, after all these years, so much interest in our music.

Back at the peak of your popularity in the '70s, what did you think the Carpenters' legacy would be 20 years later?

We didn't think about it – there was no time to think about it. But now that I've been asked that a couple of times, I can say I'm not surprised at the length of time the music has remained popular. It was never really trendy music and Karen has a timeless voice. What surprises me now, as maybe it did then, is the degree of the interest. Especially in the U.K, I hear from people just how big we still are there. There's a sound-alike act that sold out the London Palladium.

So there are Carpenter imitators?

Yeah, this one outfit sent me a DAT, and they're very good. The lady is in Karen's vocal register, and the chap has the arrangements down. I mean, I've heard some sound-alike things through the years, like this one from Japan called the "Car-Painters," and it's all off; the inversion on the intro to "Close To You," "Goodbye To Love," forget it! But these two, it's nuts on, right down to Tony Peluso's guitar solo. I was quite impressed. But I guess the whole thing continues to be a phenomenon over there.

I was told by someone at A&M that the label does three to four new Carpenters collections each year.

And I end up putting them together! We're down there right now doing a six-volume set for Japan. Six CDs! And I think, "What more could anyone want?" It's the same stuff! I just got a note from a fellow at Rondor Music wanting me to know that for the year ending 1993, the Carpenters were still Rondor's biggest selling act in Southeast Asia. I guess in a sense I have to feel a little vindicated. I'm not saying everybody should like this stuff; I just think early on we were a little unfairly treated in dismissing us as bubblegum and lightweight. I remember one British article saying "It's middle-America hokum, and I say to hell with it!" [*Laughs*] Could you make yourself a little more clear?

Will the die-hard, card-carrying Carpenters fan club member like this record?

Probably not. I could be all wrong, but I tend to be, maybe because I'm a musician, open to a lot of different sounds if they're done well and honestly. I hope the "card-carrying" fan opens up their mind and appreciates the intent behind this and the work that went into it. But I know some of the mail I get, if I just remix something, they'll say, "How could you remix this? It's classic stuff!" Well, it's *my* classic stuff!

How does it feel to be doing all these press interviews again?

I can do without it. I've said all I have to say about Karen's personal problems. There's nothing new I can add. And I want Karen to be remembered for a little more than having died of anorexia. So the only reason I've agreed to do what I've done for this is because it's more about the music.

213

This record was truly a labor of love for both Matt and I. Do you think it makes a fitting 25th Anniversary celebration for the Carpenters?

It's certainly different, fresh and inspired. And I want to thank both you and Matt for the idea and the work you've put in on this.

David Konjoyan is editor of GRAMMY Magazine, the official publication of the National Academy of Recording Arts and Sciences.

Pop Charts:
How Richard Carpenter's Lush Arrangements Turned Hit Songs Into Pop Classics

By Daniel Levitin
Electronic Musician **(1995)**

A distinguishing feature of pop tunes in the '60s was their lush horn and string arrangements. A good arrangement not only brings texture to a composition, it can also go a long way to setting the right mood and adding excitement to the tune. One of the most gifted arrangers to emerge in popular music is Richard Carpenter, one half of the Carpenters, the duo he formed with his sister Karen.

While Karen drew most of the attention as the vocalist, Richard's behind-the-scenes contributions to the Carpenters' success are immeasurable. He acted as A&R man, selecting tunes, he wrote many of their hits (such as "Yesterday Once More" and "Top Of The World"), and he played keyboards. In addition to these roles, he also arranged and orchestrated nearly all of their recorded output. It is these contributions as an arranger that have earned him a reputation among insiders as one of the best pop arrangers of all time. Five nominations for a "best arrangement" Grammy testify to this.

"The arrangement is everything," Richard explains. "No one could think more of Karen than I do, but you can have the best singer on the planet and the best song, but if you don't have the right arrangement for that song, the singer's going nowhere and neither is the song. The arrangement is everything that makes a hit record."

A good arrangement becomes inseparable from the song itself. Subsequent artists who cover such a tune find themselves keeping these arrangement ideas, because performing the song without them is unimaginable. Try to imagine the Rolling Stones' "Satisfaction" without the distorted guitar lead at the beginning, or U2's "New Year's Day" without the heavily reverbed piano intro.

What made Carpenter's arrangements so clever and musical, and how did he come up with them? One characteristic of his work is that he gives each instrument a unique place, not just in the frequency spectrum, but also in time. Featured instruments weave in and out of the spotlight, filling holes where necessary, but never stepping on each other. The different parts of his arrangements lock together to form a seamless whole.

A case in point is the Leon Russell/Bonnie Bramlett composition, "Superstar," one of Carpenter's most beautiful arrangements. The song was first recorded on Joe Cocker's *Mad Dogs And Englishmen* album with Rita Coolidge on vocals and Leon Russell on piano. But Richard first heard its potential as a Carpenters single when a then-barely-known Bette Midler sang it on the Johnny Carson show. Richard's arrangement introduced lots of new music that has become so identified with the song, so inseparable from the melody, that when people go back and hear the other versions, they're overwhelmed by the sense that something is missing from them.

Carpenter starts off with a harp glissando using the Eb (V) major scale (the song is in Ab). The gliss starts on F and ends on G a 9th above, as the strings come in on an F (vi) minor chord. Just as the harp reaches its G, Richard introduces an opening theme he wrote, played on the oboe. At first the theme anticipates the first few notes of the vocal melody which enters nine bars later, and then it evolves to an entirely new melody, a sort of variation of the main vocal line.

As the oboe decrescendos in bar 5, Richard brings in a three-part French horn line, which ends on an F minor (in second inversion) in bar 8. But you won't find this last chord anywhere but the old vinyl version of their third album; Richard recently added three more horn voices to the track using Kurzweil horns, putting the 10th on the bottom; and it is this version that was pressed onto all CD versions of the tune. "We'd play Vegas a couple of times a year," Richard explains, "and our conductor in Vegas, Dick Palombi, came up with this idea. He said, 'have you ever tried filling out the arrangement?' And he played it for me on the piano and it was beautiful, so I said 'do it!' So he wrote that into the charts and from then on – this was '72 or '73 – we did it that way. When we remixed the song for the *Yesterday Once More* album, I didn't want to hire a band just for that one chord on the remix, so I played the Kurzweil, adding it to the existing horns."

Notice next, in bar 9 [00:20 on the CD], how Richard sets up the main rhythmic theme for the song, a dotted quarter-eighth half note rhythm on the kick drum and bass, doubled on the left hand of the piano for a really fat,

216

and commanding, sound. Enhancing the fatness of the sound is the way the bass comes into bar 9 by dropping an octave – when Joe Osborn finally hits his low F from an octave above, it sounds like the lowest note you've ever heard.

This introduction to the tune is very carefully crafted to set the mood, and uses orchestral instruments to provide a lush texture. Richard's opening oboe theme is all most people need to hear to recognize the song. Two groups recently covered the song – Sonic Youth (on the *If I Were A Carpenter* tribute album) and Chrissie Hynde (under the pseudo-band name "Superfan," from the *Wayne's World* soundtrack album) – and they left Richard's intro line untouched.

Richard's use of "call and response" lines is also classic, and typical of his approach to creating cohesion between different instrumental parts. At the top of the second verse [00:52] Karen sings the lyric "your guitar" on the notes G-F-C (recognize this from the oboe intro?), and this line is then immediately echoed by the violins.

For the chorus, Richard pulls out all the stops. Hal Blaine's drum fills coming into bar 26 ("B" on the chart) are accented by Richard's frenetic electric piano fills. A tambourine plays 16th notes throughout the chorus, adding to the rhythmic build. Karen sings the first line of the chorus, "Don't you remember you told me you loved me baby," which is answered by the trumpets in bar 27 with a horn fill that is one of the most recognizable signature lines in all of pop music, filling the space between vocal lines with a bright, Tijuana Brass-type fanfare. To many, it would be unthinkable to perform the song without this line. Although Chrissie Hynde left it out, Sonic Youth kept it, transferring it to piano.

Coming out of the first chorus, a 10-bar interlude parallels the intro, complete with harp glissando [1:35] and the obbligato oboe. Notice that this second time through the theme, Richard's grand piano echoes the oboe line in octaves in "call and response" style.

Another interesting part of the track is Karen's vocal performance. Listen to the way she sings the words "far away" [from 00:34 - 00:37 on the CD] – while holding the word "away" she brings out a subtone in her voice that conveys deep and troublesome emotions. Richard knew her range incredibly well, and his choice of key made moments such as this possible. Karen was also a master at phrasing – in the subsequent words, "I fell in love with you," she sings just behind the beat – not unlike Sinatra – playing around with the time to impart more depth to the vocal.

Another of Richard's witty arrangements is the brass part for the Paul Williams/Roger Nichols tune "Let Me Be The One," also from their third album, *Carpenters*. Scored for three trumpets and two trombones, in bar 5 of the tune Richard writes horn hits on beat 2 and on the "and" of beat 3. These propel the song rhythmically into bar 6, where the usual thing to do would be to repeat the rhythm. But instead, Richard delays the bar 6 entrance by half a beat, putting the next hits on the "and" of beat 2 and straight on beat 4. This lack of symmetry takes the listener by surprise and spices up the rhythm of the arrangement. Note also how Richard voices the sus4 chord in bar 8 for a fat sound: the trombones take the root and 7th, while the trumpets cluster tightly with the sus4, seventh and octave.

Richard usually knew exactly what he wanted, and he was not afraid to be stubborn about getting it. For most of the tunes, Richard didn't just write out parts for orchestral instruments, but he wrote out all the drum beats, too – the kick, snare, hat and crash – in most cases leaving the fills for the drummer to improvise. On "Let Me Be The One," however, Richard knew exactly what he wanted. "To me, the fill [into bar 5] had to go 'tiba-dump, dump,' so I wrote it out that way."

Richard also wrote out the bass parts, and wrote out certain fills the way he wanted them, too. At first, this approach ruffled session bassist Joe Osborn. "At first Joe wasn't a big fan of mine," Richard recalls. "He was hot on Karen and just put up with me – I don't think he really wanted me around. I wrote a fill for him, note-for-note for 'Crystal Lullaby' and he looked at it and he said 'I can't do that. The bass won't go that high.' And I said, 'of course it'll go that high!' Now when he was doing the Mamas and Papas and 'Never My Love' [the Association] and 'Travelin' Man' [Ricky Nelson] and all that, he could never read a note – he was just a natural musician. And the producers would put up with him learning the songs on the spot because he was so damn good. But a chart meant nothing to him. So they'd play him the demo or sing it to him – John Phillips would play him 'California Dreamin' – until he learned it. "It finally got to him and so he taught himself – or had someone teach him – how to read. He was reading by the time he worked with us. And I'll tell you, once he learned how to read, he was among the best in the business. That 'Man Smart, Woman Smarter' thing, where it starts on the downbeat and yet it sounds like a pick-up, 'ba-bomp' – when we counted that off, and it was a room full of good musicians – the only person who came in was Joe Osborn. You know, just like the theme from *The Apartment* sounds like it's starting on a pick-up, you can't tell where the downbeat is. So we'd written out this part and he played it and of course it worked fine. And as soon as that was done, he said 'you're a genius!' And I said, 'I'm not a genius, Joe, all I did was write what I pictured you doing!'"

This is one of Richard's arranging secrets: he loves certain players, and he'll write parts just the way he imagines they would play them. For the flugelhorn solo in "Close To You," for example, Richard tried to imagine how Herb Alpert would play a part written by Burt Bacharach. When it came time to do the session, though, Alpert wasn't available so they brought in Chuck Findley. But Richard had written out the way Herb would naturally bend notes at the end of phrases [see score in bars 38-40]. "Chuck didn't play it that way at first, but I worked with him and he nailed it. A lot of people thought it was Herb – Bacharach thought so, too. But it's the way Findley is playing it."

"Arranging the ending of that tune was a problem for me," Richard continues. "I hate fade-outs and try to avoid them. Now we had the background vocals doing the 'wah-ah-ah-ah-ah' part and then what should come next? Well, again, I thought, 'how would Bacharach do this?' He often had these kinds of trick endings, like at the end of "Raindrops Keep Fallin' On My Head." Completely new music. Why is it there? Well, why shouldn't it be there? It makes it! It's a neat part. In fact, the best part of the record. And obviously, that's why we ended the song with the wahs – they're an important part of that record. Then in rehearsal, Karen came up with the idea to push [syncopate] the third one, and that is great." Of course, the Cranberries' new version of the song retains the 'wah' background vocals. How could they not?

"I never really learned how to technically orchestrate," Richard says. "There's a credit that says 'special thanks to Ron Gorow'. Ron is an actual orchestrator, and a hell of a nice guy, and he understands my idiosyncrasies and we've been working together for over twenty years. I would usually work out all the instrumental parts on a piano and then Ron would sit next to me and write down what I played! I write music, of course, but I never spent so much time at it that it became second nature the way it is for Ron. Plus, I always felt it was a bore to sit down to write out music!"

In general, Richard works from the general to the specific, sketching out some rough ideas and filling them in later. "When I'm just starting the arrangement, I'll listen to the song and I'll think, 'I want the strings to come in here.' I can't tell you at that point in time what exact notes they're going to be, but I know I want strings. I'll know also whether it's going to be a single line or a pad.

"To me, the best things are inspired things that just fall out. Of course, this goes for writing tunes, too. Nichols and Williams said they wrote 'We've Only Just Begun' in something like four minutes. And it didn't take much longer for me to write 'Yesterday Once More.' When I was arranging 'Superstar,' for example, that horn lick [sings the horn part from bar 27] was just there – I didn't have to stop and think about it. As soon as I heard 'don't you remember you told me you loved me baby' I heard 'ba-da-da-dap-da-da-da-da' in my head."

Carpenter says another crucial aspect of arranging is to pay a great deal of attention to the key, optimizing it for the singer. This means getting to know your singer's capabilities and deficiencies intimately.

In the old days, when he arranged everything on the piano, he says he would "just picture it, and cross my fingers! Now, of course, with what I have in the other room [his current home studio – see "Carpenter's Tool Box"], I can take home a rough [mix], lay down a track and futz with strings and brass all I want.

"It's so much easier now, with modern technology, because I can get some semblance of what the string parts are with my synths, even though they certainly can't duplicate them. But back then, there was nothing – I just had to envision them. There's a setting on the D50 I like called 'Arco Strings' and it's not as buzzy as some of the other ones. The buzzy ones really bug me. With the synths I can fine-tune an arrangement more. And I can get it so I know exactly what it is before we go into the studio with the real musicians. When you add MIDI and sequencers, you have a great tool. You can fiddle around with things at home before you get to the studio, and of course stuff's so good these days that if you get proficient with the equipment you can just dump it onto the multitrack when you get to the studio.

"For an arranger and a keyboardist, just having a different sound'll bring out a different emotion, maybe a different series of chord changes. I can go to a Rhodes and immediately start playing something different than I would on a Baldwin, or a Steinway, or a Wurlitzer electric – because the sound brings out something different.

"I don't like the idea of becoming fossil, because I used to be up on all the new technology. It's scary how fast things have changed. It doesn't seem that long ago that the Arp Odyssey came out. I kept mine; I figured I'd show it to my kids some day. It seems like all anybody got out of that thing was that one sound, you know, like at the end of Emerson, Lake & Palmer's 'Lucky Man': 'oo-wee-oo, wee-oo, wee-oo.'"

In summary, the key to good arranging, according to Richard, starts with these steps: (1) Find a song you really like. (2) Make sure the key is exactly right for the singer. (3) If the arrangement doesn't just "fall in your lap" through pure inspiration, build it up slowly, working from general ideas to more specific ones. (4) Weave instrumental and background vocal parts in and out of each other, and in and out of the lead vocal. Don't bury parts by having too many things going on at once. Let the arrangement echo forward and backward to other parts of the song. (5) Don't be afraid to stubbornly insist that players give you what you really want to hear.

Carpenter's Tool Box:

Richard's home studio is warm and comfortable, and is built into the bottom floor of his southern California home. Equipment includes a Yamaha Upright Acoustic ("I love these because they have the dampers, the 'apartment mode' so I can play after the kids are in bed"); Yamaha electric piano; Soundtracs 32x8x8 console; Alesis ADAT; Roland R8M and JB880 sound modules; Proteus II; Emax II; Peavy Bass module; REV7, Quadraverb, SPX900, Mac Centrus 650; Performer, Finale, Tannoy SGM10-B speakers, Alesis 3630 compressor; SV3700 DAT; Hafler power amp.

Dr. Daniel Levitin has taught at Stanford University, where he lectured on the arranging practices of Richard Carpenter in his popular music courses. Currently, he is Assistant Professor of Psychology at McGill University in Canada.

Karen Carpenter's Lost LP

By Jerry Crowe
Los Angeles Times (1996)

Karen Carpenter didn't live long enough to see her only solo album released, and it didn't look as if her fans around the world would live long enough either.

A&M Records has kept *Karen Carpenter*, a 12-song collection, locked away for 16 years. But after a 1994 Carpenters tribute album – featuring versions of the group's hits by such acts as Sheryl Crow, Sonic Youth, Matthew Sweet and the Cranberries – sparked renewed interest for the duo's work, A&M will release the solo package on October 8.

"Interest in the Carpenters has never waned; it has only varied in degree from one time to another," says Diana Baron, a senior vice president at A&M. "Since the release of *If I Were A Carpenter* two years ago, we've experienced a wave of renewed interest from fans. This record is for them."

Recorded in 1979, four years before Carpenter died at age 32 of heart failure caused by anorexia, the solo album offers a rare glimpse at a looser side of a singer best known for her ultra-sweet romantic ballads and wholesome girl-next-door image.

The collection includes three disco tunes, a reworking of Paul Simon's "Still Crazy After All These Years," a duet with Chicago's Peter Cetera and even a country ballad.

"She was one of those amazing vocal talents, and a very interesting girl – a lot deeper than a lot of people gave her credit for," says eight-time Grammy winner Phil Ramone, who produced the record. "She was really at a phase in her life where I think she was facing womanhood and... needed to expand her horizons.

"Like anybody who comes out of a group, it was time for her to express herself as a vocalist, and also to show that... maturity was setting in. The goody-two-shoes thing, I think, was getting to be a problem for her. Not on a personal level, but career-wise."

223

The album concept came about when Richard Carpenter, Karen's older brother and musical partner, announced in 1979 that he wanted to take the year off after a hectic recording and performing pace that established the duo as the most successful American pop group of the '70s.

Karen, though, couldn't imagine sitting around for a year. "It was okay for a little bit," she told an interviewer in 1981, "but then I was anxious to go back to work." She denied rumors that the album was part of a plan to eventually sever ties with her brother.

Herb Alpert, the label co-founder who had signed the Carpenters to A&M, put her together with Ramone, whose work with Billy Joel, Kenny Loggins and Paul Simon had made him one of the hottest and most respected producers in the industry.

"I thought it was strange, in a way [to be picked], because the collection of artists I was working with at the time were a little more tough and a little less middle of the road," Ramone says. "But it was her vocal ability that attracted me and made me feel that we could work together."

The producer and singer listened to hundreds of songs before selecting about 20 to record. Among the tunes that made the album were two by Rod Temperton. "It was fun cutting it and seeing that I could do all that – sing a different type of tune and work with different people," Carpenter said in 1981. "I wasn't sure if I could do it myself."

She and Ramone were happy with the initial results, and A&M added the album to its 1980 release schedule. But when recording dragged on, Richard started getting itchy to return to work. The record was subsequently shelved because Karen had decided that her work with Richard should take precedence and that she didn't want her solo record to interfere with the Carpenters' projects.

"You obviously get disappointed," Ramone says of his reaction at the time. "Timing is important on a record release. I blame myself for some of the songs sounding a bit dated now, but it was recorded at the time of *Saturday Night Fever* and all those other disco hits. When it didn't come out, I thought, 'Oh, damn. This won't have a long shelf life.'"

Richard Carpenter, who has included alternate versions of six of the record's tracks on Carpenters retrospectives, has endorsed the album's release. And even though the disco-heavy tracks seem stuck in a time warp, Ramone also is pleased to see it finally come out.

"I hope her fans will excuse some of it," Ramone says, "but I don't apologize for any of it. I know how she felt about it, and I know how I feel. I still feel good about it. Some of the songs on there are definitely mature works – and worthy of Karen Carpenter."

Album Review:
Karen Carpenter

By Tierney Smith
Goldmine **(1997)**

When Karen Carpenter began recording her first solo record in the spring of 1979 with producer Phil Ramone, the aim was to broaden her musical appeal by trying for sounds not normally heard on a Carpenters album. (Though Ramone evidently did not want to stray too far from their signature sound; lush Carpenters-style vocals are all over the place here and the overall feel is distinctly mellow.) Less-than-enthusiastic reactions from brother Richard and some A&M execs, though, convinced Karen to shelve the project.

Now that the record has seen the light of day, one thing is certain – her best work was well behind her at that point. The record does, however, have its moments. Backed by Billy Joel's band, the record's saving grace is Carpenter's always warm and expressive vocals: She brings a sweetness to the buoyant, gently ringing pop of Peter Cetera's "Making Love In The Afternoon," shines on the lovely understated country ballad "All Because Of You" and sounds right at home with the infectious mellow pop of "Guess I Just Lost My Head."

On the other hand, Ramone was obviously making a concerted attempt to steer Carpenter away from her established wholesome image (though the issue of whether the public was really clamoring to see Carpenter cast as sex siren is open to question). The results were awkward to say the least – "Still In Love With You," the only rock 'n' roll track here, is the worst offender ("I remember the first time I laid more than eyes on you" goes one line, replete with the singer's breathy little coos and tics – the effect is utterly false, as though Carpenter were forcing herself to play a very uncomfortable role.) The perky pop of "Remember When Lovin' Took All Night" and the lame disco of "My Body Keeps Changing My Mind" continues these odd, unconvincing attempts at crafting Carpenter a new image. Clearly her squeaky clean image preceded her, and rather than alter it, Ramone would have instead done well to honor it.

The real, unaffected Karen does manage to come through in the earnest tenderness she brings to "Make Believe It's Your First Time." Mostly though, she's saddled with bland, adult contemporary numbers including Rod Temperton's "Lovelines" and "If We Try." It didn't help that the fine body of work that preceded this solo effort made Carpenter a prime candidate for raised expectations.

Richard Carpenter:
The *Keyboard* Interview

By Greg Rule

Keyboard (1998)

What was the inspiration behind Richard Carpenter: Pianist, Arranger, Composer, Conductor?

I was asked by our affiliate in Japan, Polydor, to put it together. They asked for an album with piano, orchestra, and some vocal arranging after the remarkable new success of the Carpenters starting in late 1995 through '96 and continuing as we speak. Since we'd sold well over two million copies of *22 Hits Of The Carpenters*, they wanted the bulk of it to be those songs. At first I wasn't quite certain, then I got to thinking, "Well, Burt [Bacharach] is a producer and arranger. He produced records for a number of people – Dionne, Herb Alpert – and then every year or so he put out an album where he played the same songs, but reinterpreted them mostly as instrumentals.

Describe the steps you went through as you started to make the new arrangements. Was it in this room with sheet music?

It was in this room *without* sheet music. I figured out which songs I wanted. There are certain ones of ours that I didn't exactly care for as instrumentals. So I picked a number of ones I felt had a great deal of melodic sweep that would work for this approach, and a couple of album cuts such as "One Love." Then I mapped the whole thing before we ever set foot in the recording studio. Rather than record ten or 12 or however many and then say, "Well, let's see how we're going to sequence them," the whole thing was designed almost to play as a suite. "Prelude" has the bridge of the ending track "Karen's Theme." Then each thing kind of flows into the next. It was all planned that way.

Planned by mentally visualizing the end result?

Yes. I can visualize mentally... especially working on my orchestral parts. Even though I have all this [synth and sequencing] stuff, I go right back to the piano. I guess I'm just an old dog. [*Laughs*]

How did you save those ideas? Pen and paper or computer?

No. I wouldn't even know how to put it into a computer, even though I had good intentions when I got into all this stuff. But, as I've said, and as [Paul] McCartney says, "If you can't remember something that you came up with the night before, then it wasn't worth saving." And that's true! So I would store this stuff mentally and make some changes to be written later, but not the piano parts; I never bothered writing those down. I just went and played them. I wanted to record the piano first to keep everything leakage proof. Being that the music was rubato in places, I was picturing where the orchestra was going to come in, how much a retard there was going to be, and playing the piano first that way.

Not too many people can do that.

It was a bit of a trick, I'll tell you. But it worked.

Tell us about the inspiration and the creation of the song "Karen's Theme."

Originally "Karen's Theme" was a cue for *The Karen Carpenter Story.* Maybe 40 seconds long, and that was it. I always liked it. It was written in '88, and the show aired January 1, 1989. But then when the time came to put this new album together I thought, "I'd really like to finish 'Karen's Theme.'" I came up with the bridge and third verse, so it was finished. Then I got to the beginning of the album and thought, "I want to come up with something a little bit different." And I came up with the *F* minor opening ["Prelude"] and just happened to go through a *B* half diminished and *Bb* over *C*. And I thought, "Hey, I could put the bridge of 'Karen's Theme' here." That way if someone listens from the start to the finish it bookends the whole thing.

Where did you record?

Capitol [studio] A. A few tracks have bassist Joe Osborn and drummer Harvey Mason. Well, of course Joe goes direct into the booth and it didn't call for much drumming. The rest of it was just at the piano. Some of them, like the medley, start and have to go all the way through. When it got to the one rhythm part in "Superstar," the hook, I cued, the click started, and Joe and Harvey played; there's no piano on that. I just waited for it to go by, and then when it got to [*sings "dee-da-da-dee"*], click off, and I started playing again.

After the basic piano and rhythm tracks were done, what came next? The orchestra?

Yes. We did the strings separately in [studio] A, a fairly good-sized room. Then we brought in brass and wind and separated them. The percussion and the harp were done separately – all to make it as clean as could be.

And the vocal tracks were the final elements you added?

Pretty much so. There were overdubs, and of course I sang with them. I got a big kick out of doing that.

In the A&E "Biography" on the Carpenters, there was vintage footage of you and Karen recording overdubs for "Hurting Each Other." It made me wonder if you used a similar, ultra-thick layering technique this time around?

Well, it's different from the Carpenter sound, of course, because that was just the two of us. All those Carpenter vocals were sung originally two parts at a time, then we doubled and tripled them later. This was an actual studio group. It's the same type of vocal approach that Karen and I used; not a great deal of vibrato on the backgrounds. But even though it's my very same arrangement on the chorus of "Top Of The World," there's a world of difference in the sound. Both of them are perfectly in tune, but with Karen and me there's that overdubbed familial sound.

About the tour... was it only scheduled for Japan?

Yeah – for openers. We did Tokyo, Fukoka, Osaka and a number of other cities. It went very well. The crowds were great, the theaters are lovely, and the orchestras were damn good. They really delivered.

In the A&E special, they showed clips of the tour where you were playing along with a video of Karen – reminiscent of how Natalie Cole did "Unforgettable" with her father onscreen. Was that a technical pain to sync to Karen's video onstage?

No. I'm used to accompanying Karen. Of course I was also accompanying myself. So it would come up and there was a slight flam every now and again. But no, on the whole it wasn't very difficult. I just played and sang along with the videos.

Will you bring this show to the States?

Well we're working on it. I think the audience will actually get a big kick out of it. It's a lot of good music. And Mitzie and Ken Welch did a great job of putting the show together.

It was ten years between your two solo records? What occupied most of your time between 1987 and 1997?

Was it ten years? Well, working on the movie, producing other artists, working on the book, raising a family, having this house built and [preparing] any number of compilations for any number of countries. And, boom, all the time went by. I couldn't believe it. There's that old saying: As you get older the time goes quicker – which I know is impossible, but I'll be damned if it doesn't feel that way. So it's been ten years, but it's not going to be ten years 'til the next one.

What has your relationship with the piano been like through this period of time? Are you still a devout player daily?

No. I'd like to be. Again, with this, that, and the other thing I don't. Thankfully, I have a good memory, and a technique that comes back with just a little brushing up.

Looking into the crystal ball, what do you see yourself doing in the future?

Well, recording-wise I haven't thought about it yet. I think [John] Bettis and I are more than capable of writing memorable main titles for movies, things like that, certainly, and just songs. After that I would start thinking about another album, because I really enjoyed it after all that time – instead of just putting together compilations. And it's nice that the interest in the Carpenters has not subsided.

Still On Top Of The World: Carpenter Steps Back Into The Spotlight

By John Woolard

Long Beach Press-Telegram (1997)

We always knew Richard Carpenter was a good musician. But a good comedian? That we didn't know.

Kicking off his first public tour in years, Carpenter kept a near-capacity crowd happy Friday night [February 14] with his versatile performance at the Cal State Long Beach facility that he helped build and that carries his name. Those in attendance at the 1,065-seat Carpenter Performing Arts Center were treated to a show that was musically, verbally and visually pleasing.

Accompanied by a 60-piece orchestra, a children's choir and overhead photos of his family, Carpenter looked little like a man who has spent much of the past decade or so at home in Downey helping to raise a young family. Instead, dressed in a casually chic bowtie-less tuxedo with a Valentine's Day red handkerchief in a front pocket, he looked in mid-tour form. He not only performed well, but also related well to his fans.

Musically, Carpenter showed his virtuosity on the piano with deft handling of the new arrangements he has created for his soon-to-be-released album, *Richard Carpenter: Pianist, Arranger, Composer, Conductor*. Working in unison with the orchestra, he mixed in renditions of well-known Carpenters hits such as "Superstar," "Yesterday Once More," "For All We Know," "We've Only Just Begun" and "Rainy Days And Mondays" with classical pieces by Debussy and Paganini. For good measure, he threw in some Dixieland, some show tunes and a touching musical tribute to his late sister, Karen, with whom Carpenter recorded hit song after hit song in the late 1960s and '70s.

Verbally, Carpenter was at ease with the audience, and funny. He drew laughs throughout the evening, especially with commentary about his desire for a new Ferrari and – perhaps in deference to his upcoming March

tour of Japan – a routine about sumo wrestling in which he reveals his legs. Well, you had to be there.

Visually, overhead screens were put to good use, showing interesting close-ups of Carpenter's hands during such tunes as "Dizzy Fingers." They also offered up a well-produced montage of photographs of Richard, Karen and their parents, the late Harold and Agnes Carpenter. The displays were touching reminders of Carpenter's past, but those in the crowd were not drawn into a sense of pathos. If anything, it gave the opposite impression – that Richard Carpenter is alive and well and happy to be back on stage.

The most impressive part of the evening was the end, when Carpenter paid tribute to his sister, who died of anorexia nervosa in 1983. Carpenter closed with the audience participating in "Top Of The World."

"It's great that I'm up here looking at you," Carpenter said. "And it's even better that you're out there looking at me."

Credits

"The Carpenters Story" by Paul Grein (© 2000 Paul Grein. Reprinted by permission of the author.)

"Karen Carpenter: When I Was 16" by Nancy Hardwick (From *Star*, March 1973)

"The Carpenters: They've Only Just Begun…" by Dean Gautschy (From *TV Radio Mirror*, August 1971. Reprinted by permission of the author.)

"Offering" by Tom Nolan (From "The Carpenters: An Appraisal," *A&M Compendium*, July 1975. Reprinted by permission of Interscope/Geffen/A&M Records, Inc.)

"Moondust And Starlight: The *Close To You Album*" by John Tobler (© 2000 John Tobler. Reprinted by permission of the author.)

"The Grumbling Began: The Carpenters As The Enemy?" by Tom Nolan (From "The Carpenters: An Appraisal," *A&M Compendium*, July 1975. Reprinted by permission of Interscope/Geffen/A&M Records, Inc.)

"The Carpenters And The Creeps" by Lester Bangs (From *Rolling Stone*, March 4, 1971. By Straight Arrow Publishers, Inc. 1971, All rights reserved. Reprinted by permission.)

"On The Road With The Carpenters" by Digby Diehl (Originally published as "They Put Romance Into Rock." From *TV Guide*, August 14, 1971. Reprinted with permission from *TV Guide*, © 2000 TV Guide Magazine Group, Inc. TV GUIDE is a registered trademark of TV Guide Magazine Group, Inc.)

"Concert Review: Sands, Las Vegas, March 24, 1971" (From *Variety*, April 7, 1971. Reprinted by permission of Variety, Inc. © 2000)

"Rainy Days And Carpenters Always Get Me Down" by Ken Michaels (From *Chicago Tribune Magazine*, November 21, 1971. Reprinted by permission of the author.)

"Can't We Stop? Putting The Finishing Touches On A Carpenters Record" by Dan Armstrong (Originally published as "Why They're On Top?" From *Southeast News*, a Herald Community Newspaper, December 9, 1971. Reprinted by permission of Wave Community Newspapers.)

"Concert Review: Riviera, Las Vegas, September 22, 1972" (From *Variety*, October 4, 1972. Reprinted by permission of Variety, Inc. © 2000)

"The Choral Sound Of The Carpenters" by Frank Pooler (From *Choral Journal*, April 1973. Reprinted by permission of the author and the American Choral Directors Association.)

"It Happens In The Middle Of The Road: Confessions Of A Carpenters Fan" by John Tobler (Originally printed in 1974. Reprinted by permission of the author.)

"Concert Review: Sahara, Tahoe, August 24, 1973" (From *Variety*, August 29, 1973. Reprinted by permission of Variety, Inc. © 2000)

"Soft Rock And 14 Gold Records" by Frank H. Lieberman (From *Saturday Evening Post*, October 1974. Reprinted with permission of The Saturday Evening Post, © 1974.)

"The Carpenters: An Interview" (From *A&M Compendium*, July 1975. Reprinted by permission of Interscope/Geffen/A&M Records, Inc.)

"*Horizon*" by Tom Nolan (From "The Carpenters: An Appraisal," *A&M Compendium*, July 1975. Reprinted by permission of Interscope/Geffen/A&M Records, Inc.)

"Concert Review: Riviera, Las Vegas, August 24, 1975" (From *Variety*, September 3, 1975. Reprinted by permission of Variety, Inc. © 2000)

"Middle America Personified? Carpenters Fight The Image!" by Ray Coleman (Originally published as "Carpenters – Good, Clean, All-American Aggro!" From *Melody Maker*, November 8, 1975. Reprinted by permission.)

"It's An Overdose Of Pretty" by Joel McNally (From *Milwaukee Journal*, 1976. Reprinted by permission of the author.)

"Karen Carpenter: 'Nothing To Hide Behind'" by Charlie Tuna (Interview Transcript, 1976. Transcribed and edited by permission of Charlie Tuna.)

"Carpenters über alles!" by Ray Coleman (From *Melody Maker*, November 20, 1976. Reprinted by permission.)

"Concert Review: London Palladium, November 25, 1976" (From *Variety*, December 1, 1976. Reprinted by permission of Variety, Inc. © 2000)

"Carpenters' Surprise" by Ed Harrison (From *Billboard*, September 17, 1977. © 1977 BPI Communications, Inc. Used with permission from *Billboard*.)

"The Carpenters Go Country?" by Nancy Naglin (From *Country Music Magazine*, August 1978. Reprinted by permission of the author.)

"Concert Review: MGM Grand, Las Vegas, March 7, 1978" (From *Variety*, March 15, 1978. Reprinted by permission of Variety, Inc. © 2000)

"'If Somebody Would Just Let Us Know What The Problem Is…'" by Bill Moran. (From *Radio Report*, May 29, 1978)

"*Made In America*" (A&M Records Press Release, June 1981)

"Karen Carpenter Dies In Downey" by Pat McGreevy (From *Downey Herald American*, a Herald Community Newspaper, February 5, 1983. Reprinted by permission of Wave Community Newspapers.)

"Hundreds Attend Karen Carpenter Rites" (From *Southeast News*, a Herald Community Newspaper, February 9, 1983. Reprinted by permission of Wave Community Newspapers.)

"A Lesson In Art Of Emotion: Karen Carpenter's Intimate Vocals Disarm A Critic" by Robert Hilburn (From *Los Angeles Times*, February 13, 1983. © 1983 Los Angeles Times. Reprinted with permission.)

"Little Drummer Girl: Memories Of Karen" by Robyn Flans (Originally published as "In Memoriam: Karen Carpenter." From *Modern Drummer*, May 1983. Used by permission of *Modern Drummer Magazine*, Cedar Grove, NJ.)

"Karen Goes On – Thirty Minutes With Richard Carpenter" by Pat McGreevy (From *Southeast News*, a Herald Community Newspaper, October 17, 1983. Reprinted by permission of Wave Community Newspapers.)

"She'd Only Just Begun: Fine CBS Movie Tells Sad Story of Karen Carpenter" by Ron Miller (From *San Jose Mercury News*, January 1, 1989. Reprinted with permission of the *San Jose Mercury News*. All rights reserved.)

"Karen Was Wasting Away… I Had A Drug Problem… And We Couldn't Help Each Other" by Richard Carpenter (From *TV Guide*, December 31, 1988. Reprinted with permission from *TV Guide*, © 2000 TV Guide Magazine Group, Inc. TV GUIDE is a registered trademark of TV Guide Magazine Group, Inc.)

"Carpenters Telepic Boosts Records Sales" (From Variety, February 8, 1989. Reprinted by permission of Variety, Inc. © 2000)

"Yesterday, Once More" by Stephen Whitty (From *San Jose Mercury News*, October 18, 1990. Reprinted with permission of the *San Jose Mercury News*. All rights reserved.)

"Loyal Brother Brings Legacy Into The '90s" by Janet Wiscombe (From *Long Beach Press-Telegram*, September 30, 1994. Reprinted by permission.)

"That Whitebread Inspiration Came With A Dark Side" by David Konjoyan (From Orange County Register, September 11, 1994. Reprinted by permission of the author.)

"Interpretations And Vindication: The Richard Carpenter *HITS* Interview" by David Konjoyan (From *HITS* Magazine, October 3, 1994. Reprinted by permission of the author.)

"Pop Charts: How Richard Carpenter's Lush Arrangements Turned Hit Songs Into Pop Classics" by Daniel Levitin (From *Electronic Musician*, May, 1995. © 1995, © 2000 Daniel J. Levitin. Reprinted by permission of the author.)

"Karen Carpenter's Lost LP" by Jerry Crowe (From *Los Angeles Times*, August 31, 1996. © 1996 Los Angeles Times. Reprinted with permission.)

"Album Review: *Karen Carpenter*" by Tierney Smith (From *Goldmine*, January 31, 1997. Reprinted by permission.)

"Richard Carpenter: The *Keyboard* Interview" by Greg Rule (From *Keyboard*, August 1998. Reprinted by permission of the author.)

"Still On Top of the World: Carpenter Steps Back Into The Spotlight" by John Woolard (From *Long Beach Press-Telegram*, February 15, 1997. Reprinted by permission.)

Photo Credits:
A&M Records Publicity Photos (cover, 7, 17, 60, 77, 102, 159, 171, 179, 192, 222); NBC Publicity Photos (36); ABC Publicity Photo (124, 148); © 2000 Ken Bertwell (91); © 2000 Rob Autenrieth/Star Shots (205); © 2000 Ambrose Martin (234)

About The Editor

Randy Schmidt teaches elementary music in Amarillo, Texas. He holds a degree in vocal and general music education from Southwestern Oklahoma State University. Schmidt established the Newville Avenue Carpenters Mailing List, the first and largest Internet organization of Carpenters enthusiasts during its five-year existence (1995-1999). He has been a consultant for several television documentaries profiling Karen and Richard Carpenter, including A&E's "Biography" and VH1's "Behind The Music." In 1999, he served as coordinator of the Carpenters 30th Anniversary Celebration, an international multimedia event, gathering fans from more than a dozen countries in Downey, California.